CLASSIC BLACK & WHITE MOVIES

A PERSONAL REVIEW BY
DAVID KAYE

IN MEMORY OF

JEANNE MOREAU
1928-2017

===============================
© COPYRIGHT 2017 BY DAVID KAYE
ALL RIGHTS RESERVED
===============================

IN PRAISE OF BLACK AND WHITE

There was a time – long ago – when all movies were in black and white. But even in the days of silent films, color began to creep in, first by tinting the frames with a single color such as red to indicate passion or green for a pastoral setting. There were some attempts to produce a viable color film but, at that time, technology was focused more on adding sound to the movies. Once that was achieved, color was not far behind. But still many, if not most, movies were made in black and white. This was partly because of budgets – color was obviously more expensive – but even as color became more affordable, black and white films continued to be made. Even in the 1950s, when color was one of the main weapons in the film industry's battle with the new rival of television, some film makers *chose* to make their movies in monochrome. This became less of an option as the 1960s progressed and audiences came to expect movies to be in color and the studios feared dwindling profits from black and white. Today it is a brave film maker who decides to make a movie in black and white.

But the fact remains that some movies simply look better and are more effective in black and white. Just look at some of the dreadful "colorized" versions of classics such as *Casablanca* to see the truth of that. Black and white photography was a distinct art form that created a special kind of atmosphere. The *film noir* movies of the late 1940s and early 1950s are prime examples of that. Some genres, such as war films, seemed more natural in black and white. There is an old Hollywood saying that color slows down comedy films because it causes too many distractions. Who could ever imagine seeing the Marx Brothers or Laurel and Hardy in color? It just would not be the same. Many dramatic films and thrillers continued to be made in black and white because it added an edge of reality instead of a glossy veneer. True, many films required a glossy veneer but it was always nice to have a choice. Compare two Sixties spy films – *Dr. No* and *The Spy Who Came In From The Cold* – the first in color, the other in black and white. Which looked realistic and which resembled a comic book? Both were good films but would *Dr. No* have benefitted from some stylish and moody black and white photography to sharpen its impact? I like to think so.

Probably the only film genre to absolutely require color was the postwar movie musical. But they could hardly be considered realistic films. Even so, there were some very impressive black and white musicals in the 1930s, largely thanks to Busby Berkeley, Fred Astaire, and Art Deco designs.

Today, a prominent film maker such as Steven Spielberg can occasionally get away with making a movie in black and white if he feels the subject demands it. No doubt other directors wish they could as well. That is probably why so many films are being made with such dark and muted colors – they almost look like black and white – because they produce the same effect as monochrome.

We are now a couple of generations past the glory days of black and white films. Young audiences tend to avoid or disparage any movie made in black and white, even those that are recognized as classics. Perhaps they think that black and white means cheap and nasty. Well, some old movies are. But there were many great films made in black and white and this book is intended to celebrate them.

I should mention that the movies discussed here are very much a personal choice rather than a comprehensive selection. They are the result of a lifetime of watching movies and the development of my own taste in films. So the use of the word "classic" is a very loose one. To me, the movies in this book are classics but there are some alleged classics – such as *Citizen Kane* with its inflated reputation – that will not be found in these pages. Anyone who disagrees with my choices or opinions is invited to write their own book. They may find, like me, that it is quite enjoyable. But then I have reached the age where a wallow in nostalgia – especially movie nostalgia – is a pleasure that never fades.

Of course, I like color movies as well. I am a big fan of the old three-strip Technicolor process. Has any movie ever looked as glorious as *The Adventures of Robin Hood* with Errol Flynn? But as time has gone by, black and white movies have gotten a bit of a bum deal. Part of this is due to scratchy old prints with bits missing that are shown on television or cheaply reproduced videos that make them look like shadows of their former selves. With some of the modern restoration that has taken place, many old films look as good as the day they were released. Once black and white movies are seen properly they can be appreciated for the classics and near-classics that they are.

I have seen some if that most of the films in this book many times. Perhaps that is the definition of a classic – something that can be enjoyed over and over again. It would be nice if this little effort of mine encouraged someone to see a few of these films for the first time or to re-introduce them to previous admirers.

===========================

NAPOLEON – 1927

The films of the silent era were virtually all black and white. There was some color tinting along the way as well as experiments with various color processes but, for the most part, black and white ruled and audiences had no problems with that. After all, in those days, most still photography was black and white so moving pictures in monochrome were easily accepted. In any event, film makers were too involved in learning the rudiments of putting movies together to be overly bothered with trifles such as color or sound. But some of these early film makers were extremely fast learners and the art of cinema developed at a breathtaking pace.

Many people today regard silent films as somewhat primitive. This was because, until fairly recently, it was rare to see a silent film in the way audiences saw them nearly a hundred years ago. The films were not very well looked after simply because no one thought anyone would be interested in them after a few months. Bad storage and cheap film stock led to deterioration and, in too many cases, movies being lost forever. And once sound pictures came into being, interest in the old silent films virtually disappeared overnight. This was too bad because there were many gems amidst all the hastily produced rubbish of the silent era. The popular conception of silent movies is either of slapstick comedies with people like Chaplin, Keaton, and the Keystone Cops or overwrought melodramas with outrageously camp acting from the likes of Valentino or Mary Pickford. But there were also some serious, artistic and groundbreaking efforts that, when properly seen, can still produce an emotional or dramatic impact.

The best example, in my opinion, of what silent films could achieve was Abel Gance's monumental epic *Napoleon* in 1927. This massive French film – which ran over six hours in its original form – had just about everything: action, history, romance, humor, battles and crowd scenes that seemed to include every able bodied man and woman in France, and a stunning central performance by Albert Dieudonné who made Napoleon into a living character instead of a caricature. Yes, the acting style is very dated but once the viewer enters into the spirit of the film, they become lost in another world. The performances of the huge cast, with rare exceptions, are universally excellent and the attention to detail is phenomenal. At times, such as the early scenes depicting the French Revolution, the film looks almost like a documentary.

While Dieudonné dominates onscreen, it is writer, producer, editor and director Abel Gance who gives the film its style and soul. Gance was a master of the quick cutting technique and he loved jumping from one close-up of an interesting face to another to another in rapid succession or depicting action in a amazing series of jump cuts such as during a snowball battle at a military school where the young Napoleon first demonstrates his tactical and leadership skills. Gance's style influenced directors for many years and techniques that now seem commonplace were first tried out in his films.

Perhaps the most famous innovation on *Napoleon* was the use of the triptych – suddenly expanding the standard square screen into three side-by-side screens in an early example of the wide screen process. Sometimes a single image was spread across all three screens with fantastic effect while other times the two outside screens showed mirror images to complement what has was happening on the middle screen. There were originally three uses of the triptych in *Napoleon* but today only one survives – the finale as the French Army marches into Italy as the live orchestra strikes up "La Marseillaise" and the three screens are tinted blue, white and red.

Gance had intended to make six films about Napoleon to cover his entire life. Financing was a chronic problem as was the arrival of sound in 1929. Suddenly, no one cared about silent movies no matter how well they were made. *Napoleon* was chopped up and released in various versions, sometimes with a musical and sound effects soundtrack. Over the years, it disappeared which led some film historians to believe that it must have been a failure. It took British film historian Kevin Brownlow, who had extraordinary faith in what he was doing, to spend nearly thirty years in tracking down surviving bits and pieces of the film and re-assembling them.

In 1981, a reconstructed version of *Napoleon* was unveiled to considerable acclaim and began a tour of major cities where it was screened in large theaters and opera houses with a full orchestra in accompaniment. The film actually had two new musical scores. In America, the very Hollywood style music was composed by Carmine Coppola (Francis Ford Coppola had a hand in financing and promoting the film) while in the UK a more classical approach was taken by Carl Davis who worked in some music by Napoleon's contemporary Beethoven. The first time I saw the film was at the Opera House in the Kennedy Center in Washington with the Coppola score so I tend to prefer that one. I later saw a somewhat longer version of *Napoleon* in London with the music by Carl Davis which had quite a good main theme but, I felt, not quite the emotions of the American score.

Needless to say, the reconstructed *Napoleon* was not the sort of movie that could go into general release. To be seen and appreciated properly, it needs a suitably large venue with a full orchestra. So it tends to only be shown on special occasions with little rediscovered bits added. The most recent version runs 332 minutes and has been made available on DVD and Blu-Ray thanks to the British Film Institute. Of course, seeing *Napoleon* on a television screen – even a huge one – is not necessarily ideal but it may be the only way many people will ever be able to view this cinema masterpiece. It is a film worth seeing and amply demonstrates that there was a lot more to silent movies than just custard pie fights and nostril-flaring sheikhs.

==============================

RED DUST – 1932

The transition from silent films to sound was somewhat chaotic and produced mixed results as the studios jumped on the bandwagon with different recording systems. Audiences were anxious to hear their favorite movie stars as well as see them but they were not always pleased with what they heard. Many stars of the silent era were foreign and spoke with thick accents. A few, like Greta Garbo, could get away with sounding sexy but most could not. There is an old story that when Garbo's favorite screen lover John Gilbert made his first talkie, audiences roared with laughter at his high-pitched squeaky voice. This was only partly true – Gilbert was the victim of an extremely poor sound system as well as being lumbered with some excruciating melodramatic dialogue. On the other hand, both studios and audiences were pleased to discover that British stars such as Ronald Colman possessed beautiful speaking voices.

This turbulent period in film history was beautifully and humorously depicted in *Singin' in the Rain* in 1952 which incorporated some of the experiences related by old veterans on the studio lot. It was obvious that the talkies would require performers who could, well, talk and experienced stage actors flocked to Hollywood to take advantage of the situation. But audiences wanted more than perfect diction and hammy performances – they wanted stars who were real and natural. A new breed of movie star developed and two of the best of them were Clark Gable and Jean Harlow. They made several films together but none was better than *Red Dust* in 1932.

The date is significant because 1932 was before the dreaded Production Code came into being which tried to remove reality from movies and replace it with so-called family values and an early form of political correctness.

Red Dust was set in the steamy location of Indochina and had steamy situations and steamy dialogue to match. The screen virtually smoldered when Gable and Harlow were on it. Jean Harlow was a genuine sex goddess and a fairly uninhibited one at that. It was easy for her to play a woman of easy virtue and she seemed to enjoy it. Never a big fan of underwear, she moved across the screen like a cat, relishing her racy dialogue and participating in a shower scene that was deemed shocking in its day primarily because of its coyness. It was little wonder that censors, clergymen and housewives disliked her – but everyone else loved her. Her early and unnecessary death in 1937 robbed the movies of one of their brightest stars.

Man's man Clark Gable was the perfect foil for Harlow, matching her single and double meaning lines with witticisms of his own and displaying the sort of masculinity that Rudolph Valentino could only hint at. Gable was not yet the King of Hollywood but he was certainly making his mark with films like *Red Dust* in which he was the center of a fairly torrid love triangle.

Gable and Harlow dominate the film so much that it is easy to forget the presence of Mary Astor, an actress with quite a different kind of sexiness. Perhaps best known as the *femme fatale* in *The Maltese Falcon,* Astor made a number of impressive appearances in films as well as being rather notorious off-screen when, during a highly publicized divorce case, her very uninhibited diaries were leaked to the press. In *Red Dust,* Astor's quiet appeal – the tigress lurking beneath the cool façade – makes the perfect balance with her more flamboyant co-stars. The rest of the cast are merely along for the ride.

Red Dust, like many early talkies, was based on a stage play and its origins are frequently apparent. Film makers were still coming to terms with the addition of sound equipment and this affected their visual style. Cameras which had begun to move more freely in the latter years of the silent era were now more fixed which did little to disguise the staginess of the material. But the stars transcended all that and audiences reveled in movies like *Red Dust* with its passionate and slightly naughty storyline. The film would be remade in a rather sanitized color version in 1957 as *Mogambo* with Gable starring with Ava Gardner and Grace Kelly but it could not compare with *Red Dust.*

===============================

KING KONG – 1933

Compared to the special effects-laden blockbusters of today, *King Kong* – made over eighty years ago – looks very much a museum piece. So why is it still so bloody entertaining? It is possibly because it had just the right mix of ingredients with more than a little of that elusive quality known as movie magic. *King Kong* has been remade and imitated countless times over the years yet the original remains something special that continues to reward being seen.

King Kong was made during the Great Depression when audiences were only too happy to find a momentary escape from reality and *King Kong* was escapism in capital neon-lit letters. It was not the first film to feature huge or prehistoric monsters – *The Lost World* in 1925 had blazed that trail. But it was the first film to give its monster a personality.

In those dark days before computers, the special effects were primarily achieved through the laborious process of stop motion, using an eighteen inch model for Kong plus various other bits such as his face and claw for close-ups. Somewhere along the line, they managed to turn Kong into a sympathetic character and not the mindless villain that movie monsters usually were. Of course, he had his destructive moods – don't we all? – but they were usually brought about in self-defense or to protect the new love in his life, the comely and scantily-clad Fay Wray.

This updated version of beauty and the beast provides the film with much of its heart although how exactly Kong intended to express his love for Fay is left up to our imaginations. In the original version of the film, there were scenes of Kong getting quite frisky with his lady love and even removing some of her clothes. These scenes started to disappear when the movie was re-issued (thanks to the Production Code) and later sold to television and have only recently started to reappear thanks to remastered DVDs and Blu-Ray. In a nice twist, it is a human – the ruthless promoter played by Robert Armstrong – who emerges as the villain of the piece while stalwart Bruce Cabot is Kong's rival for the affections of the delectable Miss Wray.

The film moves along at such a cracking pace that there is never a pause long enough to consider the absurdity of it all. The plot is really just a series of thrilling set pieces, some of which must have scared the hell out of audiences at the time. The change of locale from Skull Island to New York City adds to the excitement, especially when Kong begins climbing the relatively new Empire State Building which was then the tallest building in the world.

Adding immeasurably to the atmosphere of the movie is the musical score by Max Steiner, one of Hollywood's finest composers. Movies had always had musical backgrounds even in the silent days when it was provided by a piano or pipe organ. But synchronized scores added to the film's soundtrack were still somewhat experimental in 1933 and Steiner demonstrated just how effective music could be in underlining the various moods of the picture. Soon movie music would be in a class all its own.

Much of the success of *King Kong* is due to its director Merian C. Cooper and his collaborator Ernest B. Schoedsack both for their vision and for their bravery in battling to get the film made. Its eventual success helped to save RKO Studios from bankruptcy, at least for a year or two. It is interesting to note that when Kong is finally shot and killed, the airplane that accomplished the deed was flown by Cooper and Schoedsack who obviously enjoyed a bit of in-joke irony. But, of course, it was really beauty that killed the beast.

I read somewhere that Jean Harlow had been considered for the Fay Wray role in *King Kong.* Now that would have been an interesting casting decision. But it is Fay Wray who will forever be associated with the creature who she described as being "the tallest, darkest leading man in Hollywood." She continued to make movies but never achieved similar success. She lived to be ninety-six and apparently did not think much of the various *King Kong* re-makes. In that opinion, she is not alone.

==============================

42ND STREET – 1933

When sound came to movies, it was obvious that movie musicals would not be far behind. And in 1933, like *King Kong,* a big splashy fun-filled musical with great songs, wise-cracking characters and lots of pretty girls was a perfect antidote to the Great Depression. Warner Brothers was the first studio to successfully jump on this particular bandwagon and they did it with great style with *42nd Street,* the original backstage musical. It must be remembered that many of the situations and lines of dialogue that seem like clichés today originated in this film when they were fresh and wonderfully entertaining.

The movie was directed by Lloyd Bacon but it was the choreographer and stager of the musical numbers - Busby Berkeley - who made the biggest impression with a style that was unmistakably all his own.

Berkeley had come to Hollywood by way of Broadway where he had choreographed a number of successful shows including some for Eddie Cantor. Berkeley's style was almost military in its precision. He had been an artillery officer in the First World War and it was said that he had become fascinated with watching soldiers being drilled on the parade ground. He incorporated this sort of precision into his choreography, moving his dancers all over the place and forming ever more complex geometric patterns with them. When he got to the movies, he also introduced what he called a "parade of faces" featuring a series of close-ups of his girls. He was very demanding in selecting his chorines and not above putting them on diets and insisting on early bedtimes. He was also a notorious advocate of the casting couch system, both individually and at elaborate Hollywood parties.

The nominal star of *42nd Street* was Warner Baxter as the harassed producer of the show that was being put together on a shoestring. The musical stars were Ruby Keeler and Dick Powell and a little way down the cast list was Ginger Rogers playing a character called Anytime Annie.

It is difficult today to understand the appeal of Ruby Keeler whose talent and appearance were slightly below that of star quality. Perhaps it was the "she's one of us" factor that audiences liked. Presumably, being married to Al Jolson, a huge star at the time, also helped to get her parts. It was to Keeler that Baxter addressed the immortal line: "You're going out there a youngster but you've got to come back a star." If she was a star – and she and Dick Powell made another six musicals together – it was only because the real musical stars had yet to arrive.

In addition to its impressive musical numbers, *42nd Street* featured another trademark of early 1930s talkies – quick-fire, wise-cracking dialogue delivered at such a brisk pace that it was impossible to catch all of it the first time around. As with many early musicals, the plot was simply something to keep the cast busy in between musical numbers and, in the end, it was the musical numbers that the audience came to see although they enjoyed a few laughs along the way ("She only said 'no' once and then she didn't hear the question.") At around an hour and a half running time, the film fairly flew by. Of course, in those days, the feature film was supplemented by comedy shorts, cartoons, newsreels, trailers and, in some of the grander picture palaces, live performances in between the shows. Going to the movies was quite an experience for just ten or fifteen cents.

Needless to say, the success of *42nd Street* led to a plethora of glorious black and white musicals of varying quality. Busby Berkeley continued to try to outdo himself with ever increasing extravaganzas featuring overhead shots of more and more girls forming moving geometric patterns set to music. Bigger meant better until the fad for such concoctions eventually faded and audiences became a trifle more sophisticated. But there is still a kind of fascination for these elaborately staged and cleverly filmed musical spectacles if only because, as the saying goes, they don't make 'em like that anymore.

The nostalgia for *42nd Street* was such that a stage version was produced on Broadway in the 1970s. It was good entertainment but it was strange not seeing it in black and white.

==============================

DUCK SOUP – 1933

It would be tempting to include all the films by the Marx Brothers in a book of movie classics but in selecting the movies for this book I decided to include what I considered to be the best representation for stars such as them, Laurel and Hardy, W.C. Fields, Astaire and Rogers, etc. For me, *Duck Soup* is the definitive Marx Brothers film. It may lack the polish of later movies such as *A Night at the Opera* or *A Day at the Races* but *Duck Soup* was the high water mark of their earlier efforts in which zaniness was unconfined and anarchy ruled as if it were a natural state of affairs.

Groucho, Chico, Harpo and Zeppo Marx came to the movies via vaudeville and Broadway. (There had been a fifth brother, Gummo, who left the act early on and became their manager.) Their first film in 1931 was a virtual reproduction of their stage hit *The Coconuts.* By the time they made *Duck Soup,* they had perfected the transition of their personalities and antics from stage to screen although it took a while for their peculiar brand of slightly surreal humor to appeal to everyone. By all accounts, the brothers were not very nice people off-screen but they were capable of making incredibly funny movies marred only by some unnecessary and occasionally irritating musical numbers.

Some intellectual observers consider *Duck Soup* to be a political satire – in that regard it was more successful than Chaplin's ponderous *The Great Dictator* – but it is more likely the brothers were only trying to be funny with this story of tiny nations with tinpot dictators. Rufus T. Firefly (Groucho) becomes the ruler of Freedonia on the recommendation of the wealthy Mrs. Teasdale (played by frequent straight woman Margaret Dumont) without whom the country would apparently go bankrupt. Naturally, Groucho is after the widow's money for himself ("Will you marry me? Did he leave you any money? Answer the second question first.") But he has a rival for her affections – the scheming ambassador of neighboring Sylvania. The ambassador enlists Chico and Harpo to spy on Groucho while Zeppo...well, Zeppo is basically along for the ride.

The film is filled with wonderful routines with Harpo on especially good manic form as Groucho's useless chauffer and in an extended sequence with Mr. Slow Burn himself, Edgar Kennedy, in which they are a pair of competing street vendors. The best scene of all is when Harpo, disguised as Groucho, crashes into a wall-size mirror and then has to pretend to be Groucho's reflection. Inevitably, Freedonia and Sylvania go to war which might not have seemed as humorous an idea in the turbulent Thirties as it does now.

Groucho gets to sing some silly songs and lopes around with his distinctive walk that resembles an arthritic banana. I think *Duck Soup* is the only Marx Brothers film in which Chico and Harpo do not have musical solos. The editing of the film is sometimes more chaotic than the action itself and suggests either changed minds or studio interference. For instance, there is a kind of *femme fatale* character played by the voluptuous Raquel Torres who seems to have been reduced to a walk-on part. The running time of the film is fairly short and probably could have been much longer if the studio had more faith in it.

What remains is classic Marx Brothers mayhem with the jokes and visual gags coming thick and fast. It was said that Margaret Dumont rarely understood lines like "We're fighting for this woman's honor, which is probably more than she ever did" and was constantly asking Groucho to explain them. Harpo, meanwhile, made Dumont's life miserable by continually stealing her wig. *Duck Soup* was the last film in which Zeppo appeared. His role as straight man/romantic lead would be taken over by the likes of Allan Jones and the unbelievably awful Kenny Baker in future films. Zeppo himself went on to have a very successful career as an agent.

Incredibly, *Duck Soup* was greeted with decidedly mixed reactions from both audiences and critics which prompted Paramount to drop them on the assumption that they had had their day. Irving Thalberg over at MGM, however, knew better. The Marx Brothers would continue to be successful but they were never again quite as zany or surreal as they were in *Duck Soup.*

================================

IT HAPPENED ONE NIGHT – 1934

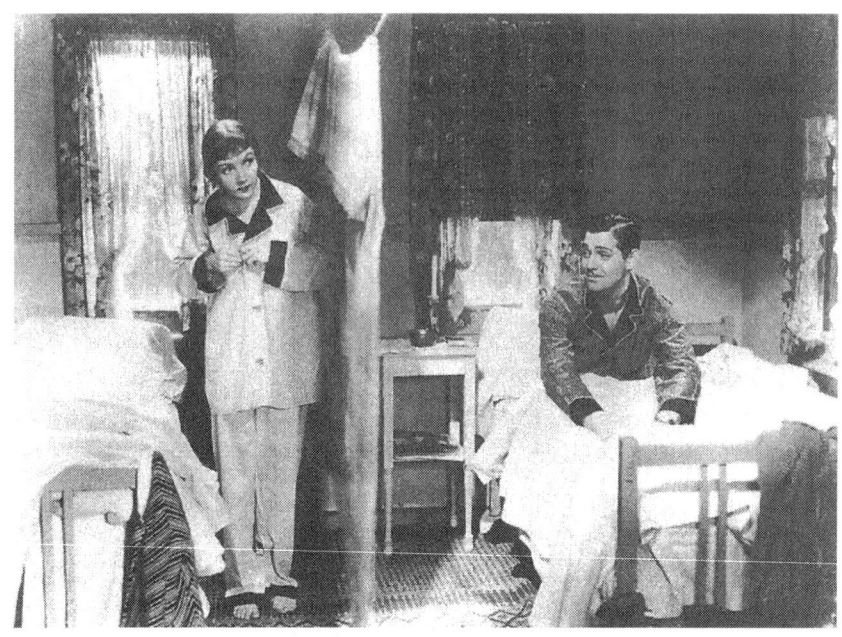

Everyone thought that *It Happened One Night* was just going to be another little movie in those days when Hollywood was cranking out films by the dozen. It was made with a limited budget and tight shooting schedule by one of the more impoverished studios – Columbia – with a somewhat reluctant cast. Clark Gable was on loan to the studio as a kind of punishment for being a bad boy at MGM. A number of well-known actresses had turned down the female lead including Claudette Colbert. But she finally agreed to be in the film after being offered a hefty salary. Even when the film was completed, she considered it an insignificant flop.

The director was Frank Capra who had not yet exhibited his social conscience with films like *Meet John Doe* and *Mr. Smith Goes to Washington* and was happy enough to helm a picture about a runaway heiress and a resourceful newspaper reporter. He had his work cut out for him, especially when dealing with his troublesome stars. Once he got into the spirit of the film, Gable enjoyed himself immensely and reportedly ruined many takes by breaking out in laughter. Colbert, on the other hand, was more of a prima donna and constantly making demands. When it came time to shoot the famous hitch hiking scene, she refused to lift her skirt to reveal her shapely leg. It was only when Capra threatened to bring in a chorus girl to act as a leg double that she relented.

Colbert clearly thought this film was beneath her. The French born star had made her name in various exotic roles including the Cecil B. DeMille epics *Cleopatra* and *The Sign of the Cross* in which she bathed in milk. Early in her career, she had been told that her left side was her best side and subsequently insisted on being filmed from that angle. Cameramen referred to the right side of her face as "the dark side of the moon." It was said that a couple of times sets had to be re-built to accommodate her wishes. But there was no time for such nonsense on *It Happened One Night*.

The movie was a prime example of everything coming together in just the right way at the right time. The Depression-era audiences loved its simple charm and slightly racy humor. Despite the odds, the two stars worked well together and managed to make the key scene of spending a night together in a motel room separated by the "walls of Jericho" into a classic moment of movie magic. The film also demonstrated the effect movies had on the public once they had left the theaters. Long distance bus companies and motels – then a fairly new concept – saw a sudden increase in business as a result of their inclusion in the film while the sale of men's undershirts plummeted when Gable casually revealed that he did not wear one. It is perhaps also worth noting that Colbert's father, played by the wonderful character actor Walter Connolly, was probably the last sympathetic portrayal of a rich man in a Capra film.

It Happened One Night managed to be a humorous love story without being overly sentimental which was a large part of its appeal. Its success took nearly everyone by surprise. It became the first movie to win all five of the major Academy Awards – film, director, actor, actress and screenplay – an accomplishment that would not be matched until *One Flew over the Cuckoo's Nest* in 1975. Of course, the Oscars are not always a reliable indication of quality but in this case they seem to have got it right. Colbert, who still had a low opinion of the picture, had to practically be forced to attend the ceremony. For Gable, *It Happened One Night* went a long way towards cementing his status as the King of Hollywood and he was welcomed back at MGM with open arms.

In many ways, *It Happened One Night* appealed to audiences, then and now, because it was pure Americana. It was not a flashy musical or a monster movie to distract audiences from real life but a glimpse of what life could be like with a bit of luck and optimism. It also demonstrated that a sense of humor was a necessary ingredient for practically any situation that life could throw at us.

===============================

THE THIN MAN – 1934

The Thin Man was another film for which the studio, in this case MGM, had low expectations. It was thought that the fad for detective stories had passed and a film featuring a sophisticated but somewhat alcoholic sleuth who was married to an elegant, wise-cracking socialite sounded more like a screwball comedy than a mystery story. In fact, it was the screwball elements that set *The Thin Man* apart from other detective movies. The solving of the mystery was rather plodding but the relationship between Nick and Nora Charles kept the audience interested. Their laidback and bemused approach to marriage – implying that being married could actually be fun – seems very natural to us today but in a movie made in 1934 it was not only a new concept but a somewhat daring one. Of course, they still slept in twin beds – you cannot have everything.

The film was based on a book by master mystery writer Dashiell Hammett. (In the completely useless information department, I would like to point out that Hammett briefly attended the same high school as me but, obviously, not at the same time.) MGM had so little faith in the project that *The Thin Man* was given what amounted to a B-movie budget and a sixteen day shooting schedule. To achieve this minor miracle, they assigned W.S. Van Dyke ("One shot Woody) to direct. He was an efficient if not always artistic director who knew how to step back and let his actors do their things.

To play the lead roles, Van Dyke wanted William Powell and Myrna Loy, two popular stars of the day. At first, MGM was reluctant to give the parts to two stars who were considered to be serious actors but Van Dyke got his way and most of the success of the film can be attributed to the interplay between Powell and Loy, with a little help from a wire-haired terrier named Asta.

The movie had its creaky moments but the stars were always there to save the day. William Powell was a fantastic actor who is largely and undeservedly forgotten today. He had an easy charm and a winning smile which perfectly suited the part of Nick Charles whether he was trading wisecracks with his wife or dealing with various lowlife with colorful names. His presence elevated many a movie in the Thirties and he was still making the occasional impressionable appearance in the Fifties.

Myrna Loy's career began in silent films where she was often cast as an exotic Oriental maiden. She was more striking than beautiful and the elegant Art Deco fashions of the Thirties looked wonderful on her. Once her flair for comedy was recognized, it was hard for her to return to more serious roles but she was always watchable.

Contrary to popular belief, the "thin man" of the title was not Powell but the first murder victim whose death Powell is called out from his cozy existence with Loy to investigate. She, of course, insists of being involved, much to Powell's annoyance and the audience's delight. The bringing together of all the various subjects to reveal the killer would become a trademark of all the Thin Man movies.

There were five further Thin Man films which became a case of diminishing returns. The best was the first sequel, *After the Thin Man,* which also featured an extremely young-looking James Stewart. The sequels were entertaining enough – a good choice for a rainy Sunday afternoon – but they never quite lived up to the spirit and the magic of the original. There was even a television series in the 1950s of an updated version of *The Thin Man* starring an uneasy Peter Lawford and a nicely exotic Phyllis Kirk. In 1976, David Niven and Maggie Smith did a wonderful parody of Nick and Nora Charles in the Neil Simon comedy film *Murder by Death* (Smith being the best thing in it).

The seemingly effortless blending of detective story and screwball comedy made *The Thin Man* a movie that can be enjoyed over and over. The movie had something that is sadly lacking in many movies today – style and wit. It does not matter if you know who did it, it was the banter and interplay between the two leads that was really what the film was all about. Powell and Loy were so wonderful together that they co-starred in a number of movies besides the Thin Man films. They richly deserved to be two of the brightest stars of the 1930s and to be remembered and watched again today.

===============================

TOP HAT – 1935

Possibly the best known pairing of stars in the 1930s was Fred Astaire and Ginger Rogers in their series of musicals of which *Top Hat* was probably the best. I say this somewhat begrudgingly because I have never been a huge fan of Astaire – I preferred Gene Kelly – but it is difficult to ignore the impact of the Astaire/Rogers movies. They, along with the Busby Berkeley films, were the epitome of black and white musicals, a genre which seemed to scream out for color and eventually got it.

Everyone always refers to Fred Astaire as the ultimate in sophistication. Presumably, this was because he wore a top hat and tails in so many of his films. But, as they say, a monkey in a silk suit is still a monkey. And my wife, who absolutely hates Astaire and refuses to watch him, always calls him "that monkey man". The British writer

Graham Greene said that Astaire was "the nearest we are ever likely to get to a human Mickey Mouse." Besides, "Fred" is hardly the most sophisticated of names.

Hollywood initially felt the same way. The report after his first screen test famously noted that he was "bald, can't act, can't sing, can dance a little." Although he had had some success on stage in both New York and London in partnership with his sister Adele, he was not obvious movie material. A chance pairing with Ginger Rogers in *Flying Down to Rio* – in which they were the second leads – led to them starring in a series of musicals with remarkably similar storylines in which their dance routines dazzled the entertainment-hungry audiences of the Thirties.

Personal reservations aside, *Top Hat* remains a fairly enjoyable film. Astaire and Rogers worked well together even if they did not always get along. Katharine Hepburn noted, rather acidly, that "he gives her class and she gives him sex." Both qualities are on display in *Top Hat* which was their fourth film together and for which RKO seemed happy to provide a sizeable budget that included the construction of an ultra-shiny Art Deco Venice that looked absolutely nothing like the real Venice. As in many of their films, the stars got considerable comic support from the genuinely funny Eric Blore and Baltimore's own Edward Everett Horton. Tossing in a collection of memorable songs by Irving Berlin completed the package.

Ginger Rogers loved her costumes and seemed to enjoy annoying Astaire with her various frills and feathers. The "Cheek to Cheek" number in particular nearly ended their partnership when Ginger's feathery gown kept shedding and getting in Astaire's face. Apparently, after that experience, he insisted on the right to approve the costumes of all her future dancing partners and he would have many including tap-dancing queen Eleanor Powell and the fabulous Cyd Charisse but Ginger Rogers would always remain his most famous partner.

Astaire did a lot of tap dancing in this and other films. Apparently, the still-early sound systems were not advanced enough to record his taps so these had to be dubbed in post-production by a little man with a hammer trying to match tap for tap. That was a good job.

Despite the romantic storylines and suggestive choreography, Astaire and Rogers did not really do much kissing and cuddling in their non-musical scenes. This strange circumstance was apparently due to the jealousy of Astaire's wife who for some reason imagined that someone else would want him. Neither Astaire nor Rogers were great singers and their acting ability was merely adequate but audiences were willing to forgive them anything once they started dancing.

Although "Top Hat, White Tie and Tails" and "Cheek to Cheek" are the standout musical numbers, I always preferred the more low-key "Isn't It A Lovely Day" number performed on a deserted bandstand to the more elaborate and highly stylized routines. All of them are impressive and certainly set the standard for movie musicals for some time to come. But while *Top Hat* can be fun to look at, it is curiously unengaging in much the way its two stars are. It reminds me of Oscar Levant's line "Beneath the phony tinsel of Hollywood lies the real tinsel." Yet it is hard to dispute that *Top Hat* remains a classic of black and white cinema.

===========================

LIBELED LADY – 1936

The Thirties were the golden age of screwball comedies and one of the most memorable was *Libeled Lady* with its dream cast of William Powell, Myrna Loy, Jean Harlow and Spencer Tracy bringing sparkling life to a typically convoluted screwball storyline in which socialite Loy threatens to sue newspaper editor Tracy for libel. In an effort to deter her and possibly dig up some genuine dirt on her, Tracy enlists his charming old pal Powell to romance the lovely lady. So involved is Tracy in trying to save his paper and his skin that he constantly postpones his wedding to Harlow who is understandably upset by the whole affair.

William Powell and Myrna Loy were an established movie couple as a result of *The Thin Man* and Spencer Tracy was just on the verge of breaking away from his various sidekick roles into becoming a headliner in his own right. The revelation in the film is Jean Harlow. Since the Production Code had made it impossible for her to continue her career as a sex goddess, she turned to comedy for which she had a considerable and unexpected flair. In a number of films in the Thirties, she was suddenly funny while still remaining subtly sexy.

Some screwball comedies have stood the test of time better than others. *Libeled Lady* remains watchable largely due to the talents of its four stars. It is one of those movies which is amusing throughout but which the viewer can seldom remember a single line of dialogue afterwards. It alternates between the frenetic scenes in the newspaper office – particularly when Harlow is present – and the more relaxed romantic interludes with Powell and Loy. It is not difficult to see why many moviegoers in the 1930s were convinced the two of them were married in real life.

In fact, at the time the film was made, it was Powell and Harlow who were an item despite an age difference of almost twenty years. The two of them had hoped to marry despite Harlow's rather disastrous track record with husbands, but her death the following year put paid to those plans. Powell was reportedly heartbroken and left flowers on her grave for many years.

It was one of the screwball elements in the film that Harlow was at all interested in the disheveled Tracy. Many people in Hollywood, even today, consider Tracy to be one of the best screen actors of all time but I have never been able to see it. He supposedly made acting look easy but he certainly enjoyed chewing the scenery in *Libeled Lady.* Still, he had a longer career than most even if there was not a great deal of variety in his roles. He is possibly best remembered for a series of pictures with Miss Box Office Poison herself – Katherine Hepburn, another name that does not feature on my list of favorites. One thing I liked about Spencer Tracy was his response to the question of why he always insisted on top billing over Hepburn on the theory that ladies should be first. "It's a movie," he growled, "not a lifeboat."

The popularity of screwball comedies lasted until the outbreak of World War Two (or, at least, America's involvement in it) although they never totally went away altogether. Many people consider *Bringing Up Baby* to be the best example of the genre but I always thought that the stars in that and similar films tried a bit too hard. One of the joys of *Libeled Lady* is that at least three of the four stars played it relatively straight. Movies like this were given a decent budget and the craftsmanship behind the cameras was competent if seldom inspired.

My wife enjoys watching films from the Thirties for their Art Deco designs and the women's costumes. In that regard, they can be a visual treat – there is more than one reason why people watch old movies.

Libeled Lady was remade in color in 1946 under the title of *Easy to Wed* which starred the strange mixture of Van Johnson, Esther Williams, Lucille Ball and Keenen Wynn. I have to admit that I have so far managed to avoid seeing this version. *Easy to Wed* has a strange claim to fame as being one of the movies on which Fidel Castro worked as an extra during his student days at UCLA.

The seemingly interchangeable romcoms of today owe a great deal to the screwball comedies of the past. They all share the same basic storyline – boy meets girl, girl hates boy, boy and girl fall in love. And why not?

==================================

WAY OUT WEST – 1937

It was not easy selecting just one Laurel and Hardy film for this collection. For many, *Sons of the Desert* would have been the obvious choice and it came a very close second. Among my personal favorites is *Fra Diavolo* (aka *The Devil's Brother*) but that probably has too many operetta numbers for most tastes. *Way Out West* edges out all the others if only because of Stan and Ollie's wonderful dance routine – and the fact that it is a fantastically funny film.

Most movie comics made a western at some point in their careers and *Way Out West* is one of the best at getting laughs out of that genre. The thin plot about the boys delivering the deed to a gold mine to a pretty young waif played by typical heroine Rosina Lawrence runs into all sorts of complications thanks to the machinations of frequent L&H foil James Finlayson as a saloon owner and very bad girl Sharon Lynne as everyone's idea of a barroom hussy.

By the time they made *Way Out West,* Laurel and Hardy were a finely tuned comedy machine with many years of experience of working together. They were among the most successful stars to make the transition from silent films to talkies when the public discovered, in addition to their usual slapstick, their distinctive voices and quirky dialogue. Stan Laurel was the creative force of the team, working out routines which were meticulously rehearsed and staying behind after filming was completed to work on the editing while "Babe" Hardy headed for the golf course. This is not to diminish Oliver Hardy's contribution to the comedy. When it came to performance, he and Stan were equals. No one was better at making an exasperated expression straight to camera than Hardy.

One of the best descriptions of Laurel and Hardy was of two very nice guys who meant well but never realized just how dumb they were. This was never better demonstrated than in *Way Out West* when they deliver the deed to the gold mine – the "MacGuffin" of the plot – to the wrong people and try everything in their limited power to correct their mistake. There are some classic scenes of mayhem including their attempts to break into the saloon after hours and Laurel being reduced to helpless giggles after being tickled by the merciless barroom hussy. Even travelling to and from the town of Deadwood Gulch proves to be an ordeal for the boys, especially when attempting to cross a river.

There are also a couple of enjoyable musical interludes. The first of these is the seemingly impromptu dance routine in front of the saloon where the boys encounter a vocal group known as The Avalon Boys who include Chill Wills who would go on to be a grizzled sidekick in countless westerns. Inspired by the song "Commencin' Dancing", Laurel and Hardy gradually turn from being appreciative listeners to surprisingly graceful performers in a dance that is the most charming and endearing Laurel and Hardy routine on film. It is impossible to watch this sequence on DVD without immediately wanting to go back and watch it again.

Once inside the saloon, it is Laurel and Hardy's turn to sing "On the Trail of the Lonesome Pine" with Stan providing more than one voice (the deep one courtesy of Mr. Wills). Most comedy films of the time had musical interludes but few were as entertaining as these. In the mid-1970s, a single of their rendition of "On the Trail of the Lonesome Pine" was released in the UK and went to number two in the charts.

French film maker François Truffaut used to say that he could not love anyone who did not love Laurel and Hardy and I tend to agree with that sentiment. I grew up watching Laurel and Hardy films and shorts on television where they were savagely butchered by the local stations in an attempt to fit them into convenient timeslots. So I am grateful that first video and then DVD have allowed us to see these films the way they were intended to be seen. After all these years, they are still as funny as ever which is a tribute to the talents of Stan, Ollie, producer Hal Roach and everyone else who was involved in making them. They are a refreshing change of pace from the aggressive and coarse comedies of today. As someone once said, Laurel and Hardy were not only a pair of gentlemen but two gentle men.

===================================

THE PRISONER OF ZENDA – 1937

At any time in my life since the age of about thirteen, this version of *The Prisoner of Zenda* would have been on my list of five favorite films. It is, in many ways, the perfect adventure/romance movie. It has everything – a dashing hero, an even more dashing villain, a lovely princess, witty dialogue, a solid supporting cast, a plot to topple a king, a superlative sword fight – all taking place at the end of the nineteenth century in the tiny kingdom of Ruritania. The original novel of *The Prisoner of Zenda* is a classic – in fact, I first encountered it as a Classics Illustrated comic before moving on to the book itself and its sequel – and it has been filmed many times, including during the silent era. But the 1937 version remains the best and is never likely to be bettered.

As much as I love Errol Flynn – and many would have thought him perfect for this film - I have always been glad that it was Ronald Colman who played the dual lead role of brave Englishman and dissolute king in *The Prisoner of Zenda.* Colman played a succession of heroes who were almost anti-heroes in films such as *A Tale of Two Cities, If I Were King,* and the non-musical *Kismet* but he was never better than in *The Prisoner of Zenda* where his mixture of urbanity and roguish charm, plus one of the finest speaking voices in the talkies, made him both a likely hero and a likeable one.

He is matched every step of the way by the flamboyant Douglas Fairbanks Jr. as the devious but ever so charming Rupert of Hentzau. Fairbanks had originally hoped to play the lead but when that was given to Colman, Fairbanks Sr. advised his son that Rupert could be quite an impressive part with a suitably flashy performance. This was more than amply supplied by the younger Fairbanks who emerged as a villain that audiences liked almost as much as the hero. It was also Fairbanks suggestion that Rupert should wear mostly black, just in case there was any doubt about how evil he was. You know you are in a different world when the hero is named Rudolph and the bad guy is called Rupert.

Helping Colman along in the madcap plot to impersonate a kidnapped king was stalwart old C. Aubrey Smith, the dean of British actors in Hollywood, and a very young David Niven as his enthusiastic lieutenant. Raymond Massey played Black Michael, the king's disreputable half-brother who sets the kidnap plot in motion in the hope of gaining both the throne and the comely princess for himself.

Princess Flavia was played by demure and very healthy looking (she played a lot of golf) Madeleine Carroll, the sort of wan and blushing princess that Walt Disney or the British royal family would have been proud of. She provides a standard sort of love interest for Colman but it is left to the always luminous Mary Astor to bring a suggestion of sexiness to the film. She had the fairly small role of Raymond Massey's mistress although you had to wonder what she saw in him. I always loved her reading of the line "You never lacked audacity, Rupert" for the way she manages to suggest an entire backstory with just a few carefully nuanced words.

The always reliable Alfred Newman provided a musical score that was by turns rousing and romantic. The steady and occasionally inspired direction was by Hollywood veteran John Cromwell. In the mid-1960s, I met Cromwell's son, the actor James Cromwell when we were both working at Center Stage in Baltimore. When I found out who James's father was, I went into youthful raptures about *The Prisoner of Zenda.* I think Jamie was somewhat taken aback by my gushing over a movie that was, at that time, already thirty years old. After all, like me, he had not even been born when the film was made.

Even in 1937, the storyline of *The Prisoner of Zenda* – the king of a tiny country is kidnapped by his evil brother only the eve of his coronation only to have his place taken by a lookalike cousin who had conveniently just arrived in the country – was a bit old-fashioned and a trifle far-fetched. But the story was told with such style and wit and uniformly excellent performances that no one seemed to mind. The story is such a classic that it has been told and re-told countless times in various media.

In 1952, MGM decided to do a full color remake that was virtually a shot-for-shot reconstruction of the 1937 version that even utilized the same music. It may have been colorful but Stewart Granger was a poor substitute for Ronald Colman and James Mason was dreadfully miscast as a very Germanic Rupert of Hentzau. The remake was, in short, lacking the magic of the original. But the source material is apparently irresistible. In 1965, director Blake Edwards devoted a large chunk of his blockbuster comedy *The Great Race* to a parody of the story with Jack Lemmon and Tony Curtis. Even worse was a very loose remake of *The Prisoner of Zenda* in 1979 with Peter Sellers in one of his weakest films. There have also been a couple of television versions as well as a stage musical called *Zenda* in 1963 that fortuitously closed out of town before its Broadway opening (they could never figure out how to have the two Rudolphs on stage at the same time).

The 1937 version of *The Prisoner of Zenda* remains a classic in every sense of the word – a little bit creaky around the edges perhaps but a creaky classic. The climatic sword fight between Colman and Fairbanks is old Hollywood style at its best with the obligatory shadows and the two combatants pausing occasionally to exchange witticisms.

Anthony Hope, who wrote *The Prisoner of Zenda*, also wrote a sequel called *Rupert of Hentzau* which picked up the story a few years later. So far as I can tell, this has never been made into a film and I am surprised that some enterprising film maker was not tempted into turning it into a kind of *Prisoner of Zenda 2.*

Just writing about *The Prisoner of Zenda* makes me want to see it again. That is perhaps the ultimate accolade that can be given to a movie – the desire to see it over and over again.

===============================

THE ROARING TWENTIES – 1939

The gangster film was a very popular genre throughout the 1930s although some of the early ones such as *Public Enemy* and *Little Caesar* now look more than a little primitive. By 1939, they had got their act together sufficiently to produce a slick movie like *The Roaring Twenties* with James Cagney and Humphrey Bogart under the skillful direction of Raoul Walsh.

Although the clouds of war were gathering in Europe, this film looked back at the violent days of Prohibition and gang warfare in the Twenties. Cagney and Bogart are among some veterans of the Great War who find re-adjustment to civilian life difficult and turn to crime instead, eventually ending up as leaders of rival mobs. Cagney was the "good" gangster while Bogart was the bad one.

James Cagney – everybody's favorite little tough guy – was the star of the film. Although he is usually associated with his gangster roles, he was actually quite a versatile actor who could do screwball comedies such as *The Bride Came C.O.D.* and lend his unique song and dance man style to a couple of musicals – in particular the ultra-patriotic *Yankee Doodle Dandy* – and even take a stab at Shakespeare in *A Midsummer's Night Dream* as Bottom. I always find it hard to believe that Cagney and not Errol Flynn was the first choice to play Robin Hood (although he certainly could not have been worse than Kevin Costner).

Humphrey Bogart had not yet attained full stardom and was still largely playing secondary roles including being the bad guy, dressed all in black, in an Errol Flynn western. Like Cagney, Bogart was a tough little guy but unlike Cagney, who made a virtue of his relatively short stature, the studios were anxious to disguise Bogart's lack of height. I read somewhere that he was the same height as Michael J. Fox but I somehow don't think he was quite as short as all that.

The Roaring Twenties was certainly a noisy film and one of the last great examples of the gangster movie whose popularity, even then, was beginning to wane. Warner Brothers populated the supporting cast with familiar faces and there was the obligatory love interest to slow things down every now and then. It is difficult to have much sympathy for any of the characters, even Cagney's more or less good guy performance. It was a rule of the time that crime did not pay and everyone ends up getting gunned down including Cagney who expires on the same church steps where Edward G. Robinson bought it in *Little Caesar.* "He used to be a big shot," his weeping girlfriend tells the police.

Warner Brothers specialized in gritty, realistic films and generally led the way with gangster movies. Many of their stories were taken direct from the headlines and the character played by Cagney in *The Roaring Twenties* was supposedly based on a real gangster – the same one that apparently inspired *The Great Gatsby.* The movies had to be careful not to glorify outlaws so real names of notorious lawbreakers were never used – that trend would have to wait until the Fifties and Sixties.

The Roaring Twenties reflected a time that was already past when the film was made. The antics of the Prohibition-era bootleggers and mobsters could be viewed with a detachment that was not possible with earlier gangster films that were made when it was all still going on. Thus *The Roaring Twenties* was not part of a moral crusade against lawlessness so much as a good yarn set in fairly recent troubled times. The gangster film would never again be quite the same as Cagney himself would demonstrate ten years later in *White Heat.*

It would be hard to imagine any of the great gangster films being made in color – black and white was the natural choice for such harsh realism even if that reality was somewhat toned down to placate the censors. The pace of those films was greatly helped by the stark black and white photography which sometimes made the movies look almost like newsreels. It also helped to keep the alleged reality from being too real.

================================

NINOTCHKA – 1939

Ninotchka was Greta Garbo's second to last film and her only comedy and as such, because of the melodramatic histrionics of her earlier pictures, is the only one of her movies that is still worth watching.

Garbo is a Hollywood legend whose career spanned silent movies and talkies where she was one of the few foreign stars whose accent was actually considered an advantage. She had a cool and aloof beauty with a hint of plenty of fire underneath. She made a number of successful films including *Camille, Mata Hari,* and *Grand Hotel* where she coined her "I want to be alone" catchphrase. She looks marvelous in the stills but watching the films can be heavy going.

This is not the case with *Ninotchka,* a charming comedy set in pre-war Paris which makes light of the East/West tensions that would later define the Cold War. Garbo's aloof manner and Swedish accent perfectly suited her role of a Communist hard-liner who encounters a feckless Parisian playboy while on her mission to sort out the shortcomings of three other Communists who had been sent to sell jewels formerly belonging to Russian aristocracy. The jewels are merely the "MacGuffin" of the plot which brings all these delightful characters together.

The playboy is played with easy charm by Melvyn Douglas who manages to turn the clash of cultures and ideology into romance. I have always wished that this part had been given to William Powell who would have absolutely perfect for it but Douglas is more than adequate and frequently amusing as he subtly tempts the Russian ice maiden with the joys of Western living.

The three helpless and hopeless Russian underlings are played to the hilt by seasoned character actors Sig Rumann, Felix Bressart and Alexander Granach who occasionally rival the Marx Brothers with their absurdity. Douglas's patron/lover and former owner of the jewels is played imperiously by Ina Claire in a role guaranteed not to invoke any sympathy from the audience. There is even an appearance by Dracula himself – Bela Lugosi – as a Russian commissar.

Garbo and Douglas provide the heart and soul of the movie with their very gradual and somewhat reluctant relationship. "Garbo laughs!" proclaimed the movie's posters and indeed she does – once or twice – but it is the witty dialogue that provides most of the fun with Douglas trying to impress Garbo with lines like "I have admired your five year plan for the past fifteen years."

Ninotchka was lovingly directed by the great Ernst Lubitsch and the equally great Billy Wilder had a hand in the script. The movie was a class act all the way and is still immensely enjoyable today.

The interplay between Douglas's shameless flirting and Garbo's cold logic could, of course, have only one result. This is, after all, a movie and it is a golden rule of cinema that opposites must attract. It is possible that Garbo found a bit of herself in the part of Ninotchka. She did not exactly melt in the love scenes even when the script called for it. One of her former co-stars put it: "Doing a love scene with Greta Garbo hardly constituted an introduction." But it is fun to see Garbo in a much more light-hearted situation than usual.

Whether she enjoyed doing the comedy or not, Garbo retired soon afterwards when her next film was poorly received. She became almost as famous as a recluse as she was as a movie star and she was occasionally glimpsed, barely recognizable, on some of the more fashionable streets of New York.

There were a couple of updated remakes of Ninotchka in the 1950s. The first was a rather limp comedy called *The Iron Petticoat* with Katharine Hepburn and Bob Hope (Hepburn was no Garbo) and then a musical take on the story starring Fred Astaire and the gorgeous Cyd Charisse with songs by Cole Porter. They both possessed only a passing resemblance to the original.

There was a kind of pre-war innocence about *Ninotchka* that added to its charm. It was also something of a fairy tale but a nice fairy tale for discerning adults. The film is also the best way to remember the star that was Greta Garbo.

==============================

THE BANK DICK – 1940

There were a number of very eccentric and almost surreal comic actors around in the good old black and white days but none was more off the wall than W.C. Fields. For some reason, it took me a long time to get into Fields and his peculiar brand of humor. I had been aware of him but had only seen him as Mr. Micawber in the 1935 film of *David Copperfield* which he lightened up considerably. I first saw a comedy short of his – *The Fatal Glass of Beer* – on television almost by accident. Fields was in a remote log cabin somewhere in the frozen north and every time he opened the door or looked out the window he announced "And it's not a fit night out for man nor beast" at which point he was hit in the face with a handful of fake snow. It was totally ridiculous and I loved it and have been a W.C. Fields fan ever since.

Fields' career stretched back through silent films and into vaudeville where he was a comic juggler with a routine he had perfected back in 1898. But he was made for talking pictures with his caustic wit and curmudgeonly attitudes. A notorious alcoholic ("I never drink anything stronger than gin before breakfast") he had a screen presence and delivery that was all his own.

By the time he made *The Bank Dick,* Fields was over sixty and very set in his ways. The film had a nominal director but it was clear that it was Fields who was calling the shots. He also wrote the screenplay under the pseudonym of Mahatma Kane Jeeves (he loved names) and played the lead role of professional layabout and reluctant hero Egbert Sousè.

The plot of *The Bank Dick* is marginally more coherent than in some other Fields features but it is the great man and his performance that really counted. After inadvertently foiling a robbery, Field was rewarded with the job of security guard at the local bank. Putting Fields in a position of authority was not necessarily a good idea. He had the usual family problems – a shrewish wife, a pretty lovesick daughter and her naïve boyfriend – as well as conmen, a bank inspector and returning bank robbers. Fields either complicates these situations or avoids them altogether with extended drinking sessions at the Black Pussy Café where the bartender was Shemp Howard, brother of Moe and sometime Stooge.

The Production Code censors, who always carefully scrutinized everything by Fields, were not happy with the name of this bar. Fields pointed out that there was a bar in Los Angeles with the same name but the censors insisted on adding "Cat" to the joint's name although Fields still called it the Black Pussy in his dialogue.

It is probably safe to assume that the humor of W.C. Fields is an acquired taste and does not appeal to everyone. By all accounts, he was not an easy person to work with but then anyone who hates little children and dogs cannot be all bad. One observer noted: "His main purpose seemed to be to break as many rules as possible and cause the maximum amount of trouble for everybody." So it is little wonder that Fields received renewed recognition and popularity among the youth of the 1960s. He would no doubt have hated the hippies but they seemed to love him.

In *The Bank Dick,* Egbert Sousè was free of every virtue. He drank, smoked, lied, cheated, hated children, old ladies and pillars of society. He was opposed to work, thrift and honesty. And yet he is somehow the most likeable character in the picture. "Never give a sucker an even break" was both his philosophy and the title of one of his films. Fields was extremely quotable, both onscreen and off, and perhaps rivalled only by Groucho Marx in that department. The amazing thing is how few of his maxims have become dated over the years. One of my favorite Fields observations is: "Women are like elephants. I like to look at them but I wouldn't want to own one."

The Bank Dick routinely makes it onto lists of the best comedies ever made. Along with *It's A Gift,* it probably represents the high point of Fields' career although many of his shorts, especially when playing a dentist, golfer or pool shark, are definite classics. It is no small accomplishment that we can still laugh out loud at movies made over seventy-five years ago.

==============================

REBECCA – 1940

After directing a string of successful British thrillers, Alfred Hitchcock was invited to Hollywood to direct the film version of Daphne du Maurier's best-selling novel *Rebecca.* It was perhaps a logical move as the war in Europe had just begun and it was unlikely that Hitchcock would be pursuing his career in Britain for a few years. As it turned out, he stayed more or less permanently.

Rebecca may come as something of a surprise to viewers who associate Hitchcock with some of his later films such as *North by Northwest, Psycho,* and *The Birds.* This was much more a psychological and somewhat subtle thriller in which an extremely naïve young woman marries a dashing widower after a whirlwind romance, then settles down to life at his country estate where she is constantly confronted with reminders of his dead wife.

Her situation is not helped by the malevolent housekeeper who seems obsessively loyal to her former mistress. The housekeeper, Mrs. Danvers, was played with menacing gusto by Judith Anderson, a classical stage actress who had triumphed in roles such as Medea and Lady Macbeth. In *Rebecca,* she manages to stay just this side of pure evil as one of the scariest characters to ever appear in a Hitchcock film.

The nameless young bride was played by wan and whimpering Joan Fontaine who seemed to specialize in roles requiring excessive timidity. She got the part by beating out a number of other actresses including Vivien Leigh and her older sister Olivia de Havilland, someone she never particularly got along with anyway. The role of handsome but mysterious Maxim de Winter went to Laurence Olivier, who was not yet a household name, after first choice Ronald Colman turned it down.

Olivier was fresh from his success in *Wuthering Heights* and had hoped to co-star in *Rebecca* with his mistress and future wife Vivien Leigh. When Fontaine got the part instead, he was reportedly not very nice to her and apparently whispered obscenities into her youthful ear during their love scenes which produced somewhat shocked expressions that Hitchcock loved. In general, Fontaine was made to feel uncomfortable on the set in an effort to aid her performance as a woman on the verge of a nervous breakdown.

Alfred Hitchcock was famously misquoted as saying that actors were cattle. What he actually said was that they should be treated like cattle. His direction of actors mainly consisted of telling them where to stand or where to move but next to nothing about their performances. If someone asked about things like motivation, Hitchcock merely shrugged and replied: "It's only a movie."

Rebecca won the Academy Award for best picture – the only one of Hitchcock's films to do so. He himself, despite his long career, many successes, and influence on other directors, never got the best director award. It is a puzzle because *Rebecca* is among his finest work with its brooding gothic atmosphere and undertones of menace. It is also, unless I am mistaken, the only Hitchcock movie in which the Master does not make one of his trademark cameo appearances. Apparently the bit was shot but failed to make the final cut.

This was a prestige production overseen by the great David O. Selznick and it looked it with fantastic black and white photography and a suitably somber musical score by Franz Waxman. Playwright Robert E. Sherwood worked on the script and a solid supporting cast of recognizable faces, including George Sanders, helped to keep the story moving. Of course, this being a Hollywood production, the ending was given a slightly happier twist than the one in the book but no seemed to mind.

Alfred Hitchcock would go on to have a long and colorful career in Hollywood. He is one of the very few movie directors whose name would inspire people to buy tickets to see his latest film. Most movie goers who are not dedicated film fanatics would be hard pressed to name more than a couple of movie directors – at least in the days before Lucas and Spielberg – but Hitchcock is always one of those names. This is partly due to the quality of his work and partly the result of his own shameless self-promotion. When we watch a film like *Rebecca,* we are seeing Fontaine and Olivier but we are always aware that it was Hitchcock behind the camera.

==================================

THE SEA HAWK – 1940

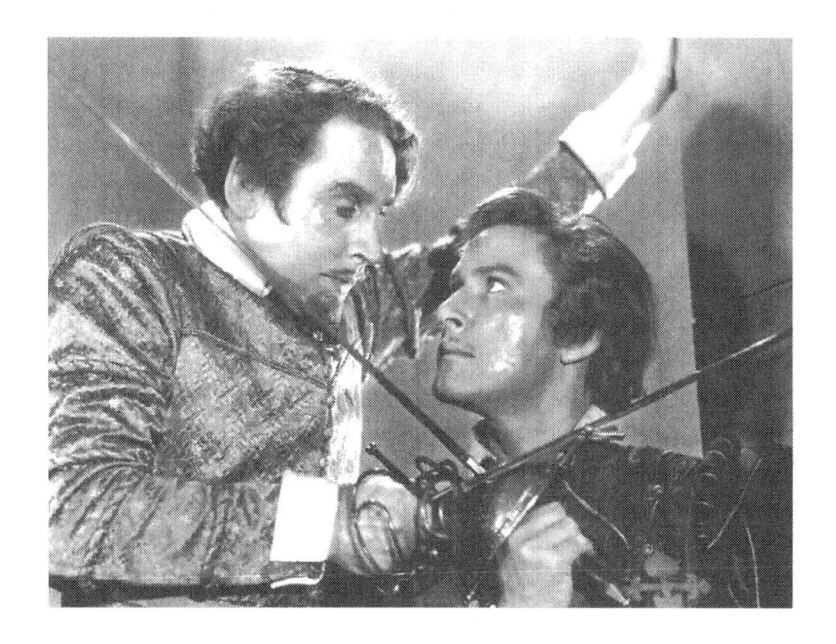

Errol Flynn was my first real movie hero. During the summer when I was about ten or eleven, one of the local TV stations had an Errol Flynn week on their afternoon movie. While the other kids played outside, I sat transfixed by this dashing figure in a way that might have worried a psychiatrist or two. Flynn was what they called devilishly handsome. His limited acting ability was more than compensated by his good looks and natural athleticism. A notorious life off-screen did not hurt his reputation either. He could play various roles ranging from westerns to historical epics in which he made misunderstood heroes out of the likes of George Armstrong Custer and the Light Brigade. He was even briefly in the running to play Rhett Butler in *Gone with the Wind.* But it was as a swashbuckler that he will always be best remembered and he was never better than in *The Sea Hawk.*

Flynn's first swashbuckling success, *Captain Blood,* had taken everyone by surprise but by the time *The Sea Hawk* was released they knew what to expect. Warner Brothers knew they were on to a good thing and assigned some of their top people to the production, in particular director Michael Curtiz and composer Erich Wolfgang Korngold whose magnificent score is one of the very best of that era of great film music. Michael Curtiz was a very talented Hungarian-born director whose fractured English frequently amused both cast and crew of his pictures ("The next time I send a dumb son of a bitch to do something, I go myself."). He could direct anything including comedies and musicals but he had a real knack for bringing action and adventure stories to the screen. *The Sea Hawk* is a fine example of this with its sweeping mixture of pageantry, romance and violence.

Although there were some good choices in the casting department, in particular Flora Robson as a believable Elizabeth I, it was here that there were some disappointments for dedicated Flynn watchers. Claude Rains and Henry Daniell made a fine pair of villains but Basil Rathbone was sadly missed, especially in the climatic duel where Daniell had to be extensively doubled by someone who actually knew how to use a sword. Even worse was the absence of usual love interest Olivia de Havilland – she made a total of eight films with Flynn – and the casting of the rather vacuous Brenda Marshall in her place. Flynn may have been happy enough with Marshall off-screen but there was a lack of chemistry in their scenes together.

The storyline was a familiar one with a handful of English sea captains standing up to the might of the aggressive Spanish empire – a possible allegory for what was happening in Europe at the time of filming. Some of Flynn's adventures were based on the exploits of famed privateer Henry Morgan but most of it is pure Hollywood hokum designed to allow the inclusion of exciting battle scenes and to show off the "magnificent male animal" that was Flynn.

Viewers of more recent epics such as *The Pirates of the Caribbean* would no doubt be surprised that a yarn like *The Sea Hawk* was filmed in black and white. But the cinematography is one of the film's virtues as well as allowing the use of footage from earlier movies. Back in 1940, very few people would complain that a picture like this was filmed in black and white because it was done so well and actually enhanced the overall atmosphere of the film. At just over two hours' running time, *The Sea Hawk* rattled along nicely, pausing only for Flynn to whisper sweet nothings in Brenda Marshall's ear.

Along with *The Adventures of Robin Hood* – one of the best and most glorious Technicolor movies – *The Sea Hawk* saw Errol Flynn at the top of his power and his popularity. The effects of his "wicked, wicked ways" had not yet become visible and his sort of movies were still in demand at the box office. His decline was steady and he ended up playing parodies of himself in films such as *The Sun Also Rises* (having said that, he was the best thing in that movie). He died too young at fifty with apparently very few regrets. "I've had a hell of a lot of fun and I've enjoyed every minute of it," he remarked.

In many ways, *The Sea Hawk* is the ultimate swashbuckling movie which produced a genuine sense of adventure and gave the world a fantastic, if flawed, hero.

==============================

THE GHOST BREAKERS – 1940

The Ghost Breakers may not seem an obvious choice as a movie classic but it is my favorite Bob Hope film and has the added advantage of still being as highly enjoyable today as it was when it was first released. The movie was quickly made as a follow-up to the previous year's surprise hit *The Cat and the Canary* in which Hope had also starred with the delectable Paulette Goddard in a slightly scary old dark house type comedy. Many people rave about *The Cat and the Canary* but I always found it somewhat tame, especially in comparison to *The Ghost Breakers.*

The movie was directed by comedy veteran George Marshall and loosely based on an old stage play. Hope played a radio personality called Larry Lawrence who specialized in exposés about gangsters. On a dark and stormy night in a New York hotel, he encounters

Goddard who is about to depart for Cuba to inherit a spooky old castle. After some veiled threats and a murder, they manage to get on the boat to Cuba, ably assisted by Hope's valet, Willie "Sleep and Eat" Best in a politically incorrect role that would never make it onto the screen these days ("He sees the darker side of everything. He was born during a total eclipse."). Once in Cuba, they waste no time in going to the castle to encounter ghosts, zombies, and ideal situations for comedy and Hope's one liners.

There is a better than usual supporting cast for this type of picture including Paul Lukas, Richard Carlson, and a very young Anthony Quinn as twin brothers. It would also seem that there was some sort of subplot involving veteran character Lloyd Corrigan but despite his several appearances, nothing comes of it and presumably was written or edited out of the final cut.

Bob Hope apparently had great affection for this movie because his character was not as cowardly as usual and was actually fairly heroic at times, if somewhat reluctantly. Groucho Marx once complained that all Hope ever did was say the lines that a team of writers had provided him with. But Hope was an accomplished comic actor who could deliver those lines like no one else and had developed a screen personality that was as likeable as it was enjoyable – and he has some great lines in *The Ghost Breakers* ("I don't mind dying but I hate the preliminaries."). It was unfortunate that his reputation eventually suffered after a string of terrible movies in the Sixties.

Paulette Goddard was seldom lovelier or more enjoyable than in *The Ghost Breakers* and she and Hope made a great team. Goddard had an interesting career – she was on the short list to play Scarlett O'Hara until Vivien Leigh came along – without ever quite reaching the top tier. She was amazingly eclectic in choosing husbands – Charles Chaplin, Burgess Meredith and Erich Maria Remarque – and she was known around town as a carefree and slightly naughty girl. My favorite story about her was when she was in the running for a part in a Cecil B. DeMille film and was called in to see the great director. It was an open secret in Hollywood that DeMille had a raving foot fetish (just look at how many barefoot women are in his films) so Paulette went into his office and promptly slipped off her shoes and popped her bare feet up on his desk. Needless to say, she got the part.

It is strange to think of Hollywood producing such light concoctions as *The Ghost Breakers* when there was a major war raging in Europe and elsewhere. Perhaps it was a last attempt to have some fun before the inevitable or simply trying to carry on with business as usual. Comedy, after all, is supposedly the best medicine.

Most screen comics eventually make a haunted house type comedy sooner or later but none were better or have worn so well as *The Ghost Breakers.* It was sort of remade in 1953 as a vehicle for Dean Martin and Jerry Lewis called *Scared Stiff* but the two of them together could never be anywhere as good as one Bob Hope. Interestingly, the later film was also directed by George Marshall and Hope made a cameo appearance with his good buddy Bing Crosby.

The Ghost Breakers may not be an absolute classic but it is a very funny film featuring Bob Hope at the peak of his powers. And the crisp black and white photography is perfect for the film's combination of chills and comedy.

==============================

THE MALTESE FALCON – 1941

The first time you see *The Maltese Falcon* is to find out what the plot is all about and who did what. But on repeated viewings – and *The Maltese Falcon* is one of those rare films that rewards being seen multiple times – you can appreciate and savor all those ingredients that make *The Maltese Falcon* such a fantastic film. It is based on a novel by Dashiell Hammett and had been filmed twice before with mixed results, although the 1931 version had the advantage of being made in the more permissive pre-Production Code days.

Like many classics, *The Maltese Falcon* started out as just another picture on the production line and one that had a first-time director in John Huston. It was considered so insignificant that big star George Raft turned down the part of Sam Spade, leaving the way clear, not for the first time, for Humphrey Bogart to take over. Raft's refusal was every moviegoer's gain as Bogart proved to be the ultimate hard-boiled private detective against whom all others would be measured. *The Maltese Falcon* was the film that secured his star status forever.

In addition to directing, Huston also wrote the script, sticking closer to the source material than the earlier film versions had done. He used Hammett's dialogue and his own visual sense to bring a colorful collection of characters to life and assembled a first-rate cast to play them. These included the amazingly effete Peter Lorre, the rotund Sydney Greenstreet in his first film, smart and sassy Lee Patrick, and the very eccentric character actor Elisha Cook Jr. Best of all was *femme fatale* Mary Astor in her finest and most subtly sexy role as the mysterious woman who starts the whole plot rolling. She played the kind of broad that no one trusted but everyone wanted anyway. Her scenes with Bogart help to ignite the film rather than slow it down.

As for Bogart, he is the film and is seldom off the screen. He is coolly calculating and full of confidence as he deals with crooks, cops and women. A subplot involving the wife of his recent deceased partner seems strangely unnecessary but what is a detective story without a red herring or two? Bogart's private eye seems to know just the right way to deal with each of the characters he encounters during his investigation and, in the end, he can be relied on to do the right thing.

The combination of Bogart and Huston's talents make *The Maltese Falcon* memorable. The one could not have done it without the other or, at least, not as well. It was an early example of *film noir* and would have been ruined by color. Huston created the perfect atmosphere for Sam Spade and Bogart lived in it. *The Maltese Falcon* is always interesting visually and it is the sort of movie that audiences watch in silence for fear of missing something. It is perhaps surprising, considering what a classic film it is, that *The Maltese Falcon* failed to win any Academy Awards. But then this is a movie that deserves more than awards – it deserves to be seen.

Despite all the talent involved, they did not necessarily get everything right the first time around. The initial preview audiences had a somewhat mixed reaction, mostly because they found the movie a tad confusing. So Bogart had to be recalled from his next picture and a few additional scenes were shot and inserted. The result was the movie that we know and love today.

Peter Lorre and Sydney Greenstreet proved to be such a successful, if unlikely, pairing that they made several more movies together including taking the lead roles in the wonderful *The Mask of Dimitrios.* And Greenstreet later joined Bogart and Astor to work for John Huston again in *Across the Pacific.* Bogart, of course, had a long and busy career until cancer caught up with him at the age of fifty-seven. As an actor, he was not always impressed by some of the films he had been in but he pronounced himself pleased with and even proud of *The Maltese Falcon.*

Bogart was another movie star who posthumously struck a chord with a younger generation, particularly in the Sixties when his anti-hero persona appealed to a new and rebellious audience. It is unlikely he will ever be forgotten and *The Maltese Falcon* is a great way to remember him.

==============================

NOW, VOYAGER – 1942

Now, Voyager is one of those movies where tissues and handkerchiefs are almost as essential for the viewer as popcorn. It is the ultimate Bette Davis weepie – a vehicle perfectly suited to her particular talents. Bette Davis was no one's idea of a typical movie star. She did not look like a movie star and she did not act like one but she was someone it was impossible to ignore. She was not the first choice to star in *Now, Voyager* but she launched a fierce campaign to land the role and then proceeded to re-write much of her character's dialogue. Just before shooting began, director Irving Rapper received a letter from Barbara Stanwyck which read, in part: "You are going to do a picture with Bette Davis? Don't you know there are such things as fresh air and sunshine?"

The storyline was fairly typical of "women's" pictures of the time. A mousy spinster, after years of being dominated by a tyrannical mother, undergoes a seemingly miraculous transformation after a few months of therapy with a kindly psychiatrist, goes to Rio and falls in love with, of course, a married man.

The man in question was played by Paul Henreid who always struck me as an odd choice to be the leading man in this or any film. He was a reasonably good looking Austrian with an accent that could, to American ears, pass for just about anything. He had a strangely stiff screen presence. One contemporary noted that Henreid "looks as though his idea of fun would be to find a nice cold damp grave and sit in it."

Henreid will be forever remembered for the way he lit two cigarettes at once then handed one to Davis and kept the other for himself. It was considered so romantic that for years afterwards he was pestered by women wanting him to do it for them. It was a very memorable moment although the anti-smoking brigade would never allow such a thing today.

Also making their presence felt in the cast was Claude Rains – one of Davis's favorite co-stars – as the psychiatrist and Gladys Cooper as the dragon of a mother. But the film belongs to Bette Davis who relished the transformation from ugly duckling to chic woman of the world, getting the maximum audience reaction from carefully delivered lines like "No one ever called me darling before."

The proceedings are greatly aided by a lush musical score by Max Steiner whose love theme became a popular song called "It Can't Be Wrong" which conjures up images of two cigarettes being lit all on its own.

David was apparently not overly impressed by the music as she felt it interfered with her performance and that she was more than capable of producing the required emotional responses on her own. But the love theme from *Now, Voyager* was a melody that would be forever associated with her.

In case anyone was wondering, the film's title comes from a line in a Walt Whitman poem: "Now, Voyager, sail thou forth, to seek and find."

For nearly two hours, the movie follows Davis on her emotional rollercoaster until the final scene with Henreid, another lighting of cigarettes, and Davis softly speaking one of her most famous lines: "Oh, Jerry, don't let's ask for the moon – we have the stars." At which point virtually all the tissues and hankies in the audience come out. I would imagine the effect would be even worse on a single woman watching the movie alone on television.

Bette Davis did not have a monopoly on weepies – they made dozens of them back in those days – but she was certainly the best at doing them. As her one-time husband Gary Merrill put it: "Whatever Bette had chosen to do in life, she would have had to be the top or she couldn't have endured it." Davis herself expressed a similar sentiment when she said: "If Hollywood didn't work out, I was all prepared to be the best secretary in the world."

Just about everybody, except possibly Joan Crawford, was glad that Hollywood worked out for Bette Davis. She has given us many wonderful movie moments.

===============================

THE ROAD TO MOROCCO – 1942

The Road to Morocco is generally considered to be the best of the seven *Road to...* movies that starred Bing Crosby, Bob Hope and Dorothy Lamour. It all started in 1940 with *The Road to Singapore* for which Crosby and Hope were the third choice for the lead roles (with, for the only time, Hope being billed below Lamour). This established the basic premise for the series and was quickly followed by *The Road to Zanzibar.* By the time *The Road to Morocco* was made, all the pieces were firmly in place and everything came together perfectly.

As usual, Crosby and Hope were a pair of conmen with Crosby being the smart one who would sell out his partner for a dollar or a dame. He sells Hope to some nasty looking Arabs only for Hope to end up in the arms of a beautiful princess played by luscious Lamour.

The *Road to...* pictures were a delightful combination of comic situations, crackling dialogue, and a few songs. While there was an official script, Crosby and Hope – who both had successful radio shows at the time – had their own writers provide them with much of the trademark one-liners and gags that are a hallmark of these films. It was reported that the actual script writers, credited as Frank Butler and Don Hartman, were prone to calling out "Bingo!" when they heard one of their lines being used. But they were no doubt responsible for the talking camel who announced: "This is the screwiest picture I was ever in."

The Road to Morocco was also blessed with a better than average collection of songs, courtesy of Johnny Burke and Jimmy van Heusen, including the bouncy title number and the romantic "Moonlight Becomes You" which quickly became a standard. The art department made some nice contributions as well with exotic costumes and a shiny palace garden that looked like the set for an Astaire/Rogers number. For the desert scenes, they went to Hollywood's favorite desert in Arizona.

But, of course, it was the stars that made the movie. For me, Bob Hope was always the main reason for seeing the *Road to...* films and he was on top form in all of them. He was always in competition with Crosby for the affections of Lamour, and usually lost out to him, but in *The Road to Morocco* he managed to get a girl of his own, the exotic Dona Drake, an actress with a strange background.

Bing Crosby was not as a good a comedy actor but he was there to sing most of the songs. He was very popular at the time (my mother absolutely loved him) but some viewers today tend to fast forward during his numbers. I cannot imagine what Lamour saw in him.

When I was a kid watching these movies on television, I always considered Dorothy Lamour to be someone I had to put up with in order to get to the good stuff. As I got older, I realized how sexy she was. She had originally found fame playing exotic maidens in various movies such as *The Hurricane* and *The Jungle Princess* for which she became known as Hollywood's Sarong Girl. She could sing and dance and was a surprisingly good comic foil for the two guys – and looked great doing all of it.

For the most part, *The Road to Morocco* and the other "Road" pictures have held up remarkably well. Possibly because of their settings, they have not visually dated and the dialogue, except for a few then-topical references, remains just as sharp and funny today.

The series continued with *The Road to Utopia* in 1945, *The Road to Rio* in 1947, and *The Road to Bali* in 1952. *Bali* was the only one made in color and was made in part by Crosby and Hope's production companies. It has since fallen into public domain so beware of shoddy DVD versions. In 1962, the series was revived with *The Road to Hong Kong* which was cheaply made in England and saw Joan Collins replacing Lamour as the female lead although Lamour had a cameo part for old time's sake. This final *Road* movie was not as bad as some people claim but Crosby in particular was really beginning to show his age.

The Road to... films were very popular and were the most commercially successful film series until a chap named James Bond came along. *The Road to Morocco* is the gem among them. If you are only going to see one *Road* picture – why would you? – it should be *The Road to Morocco*.

===============================

CASABLANCA – 1942

Well, what can I possibly say about *Casablanca* that has not already been said? It is quite simply one of the best movies of all time. It is also, when seen in a properly restored version, one of the most satisfying films to watch. Some people watch *Star Wars* or *The Sound of Music* umpteen times – I'll stick with *Casablanca.*

The amazing thing is that such a fantastic film could have been created out of so much chaos. Despite its stellar participants, it was considered by Warner Brothers to be a fairly routine picture and a romantic one at that until events unfolding in World War Two gave it an added edge. The script, which went through many changes and many writers, was based on a stage play that had hardly been a success. The final screenplay was credited to twin brothers Julius and Philip Epstein along with Howard Koch and ended up winning an Oscar. But even after the film became a success, Julius Epstein regarded it as nothing more than a routine assignment. Among the many *Casablanca* legends was that the script was put together as they filmed and that no one knew how it would end. That was only partly true.

Among the other *Casablanca* myths was that Ronald Reagan was originally set to star in the film. That was simply a rumor put out by the publicity department to get the future president's name in the papers. Producer Hal Wallis had wanted Humphrey Bogart to play Rick from the very beginning even though that great also-ran George Raft had expressed an interest in the part.

Bogart was joined by Ingrid Bergman and Paul Henreid but none of them were overly thrilled to be in the movie. Bergman thought is it insignificant fluff with terrible dialogue and Henreid, fresh from his success in *Now, Voyager* (1942 was a good year for him) was not happy to be in what he considered a supporting role. And there were some wonderful supporting players in the picture, especially Claude Rains as the wily and amoral prefect of police. Bogart's co-stars from *The Maltese Falcon* Peter Lorre and Sydney Greenstreet were also there although they had no scenes together while Conrad Veidt made a suitably despicable Nazi and veteran S.Z. "Cuddles" Sakall provided some lighter moments. There was even a small part for Jack L. Warner's stepdaughter Joy Page as a Bulgarian refugee with a moral dilemma.

Someone who will always be associated with *Casablanca* was singer Dooley Wilson who got to sing the most famous version of "As Time Goes By" to tug at everyone's heart strings. Wilson's character of Sam was supposed to be a piano player but Wilson himself was a drummer and had to mime his movements on the keyboard. "As Time Goes By" was not a new song and the film's composer Max Steiner hated it and wanted to replace it with a composition of his own. Luckily for romantics everywhere, he did not get his way.

The film was directed by the irrepressible Michael Curtiz who is responsible for much of the picture's style as is the amazing black and white photography that seems to shimmer in some scenes then plays games with light and shadows in others. Considering that the film was supposed to be set in Morocco but was filmed on sound stages and back lots using left over scenery from previous movies, *Casablanca* looks pretty good.

Casablanca probably has more famous lines of dialogue than any other movie including "Here's looking at you, kid", "I stick my neck out for nobody", "Round up the usual suspects", "Of all the gin joints in all the towns in all the world, she walks into mine" and a pair that are quite frequently quoted incorrectly: "I think this is the beginning of a beautiful friendship" and "Play it, Sam". There is also the occasional line that almost causes a chuckle or two at its absurdity such as "Victor, please don't go to the underground meeting tonight."

Apparently, a few years ago, Madonna wanted to re-make *Casablanca* with herself and Ashton Kutcher in the leads but no one was interested. There has also been a couple of television series based on *Casablanca* including one in the 1950s and a later one starring the woefully inadequate David Soul. *Casablanca* was a one-off – it can never be duplicated. It may have been set in the 1940s but its appeal is timeless.

===================================

ARSENIC AND OLD LACE – 1944

The charming story of two spinsters in Brooklyn who make a hobby of poisoning lonely old men and burying them in the cellar with the help of their brother who thinks he is Teddy Roosevelt. On Halloween, they are visited by their two nephews – Mortimer, the good one, who has just married the girl next door after a prolonged courtship and Jonathan, the bad one, who arrives after a long absence with his partner in crime, the malevolent Dr. Einstein. Throw in a couple of Irish cops and the head of the local asylum and you have the ingredients for swiftly paced, slightly dark comedy that has delighted audiences for seventy-five years.

Based on a long running Broadway play, adapted by the Epstein brothers, and directed by Frank Capra, *Arsenic and Old Lace* is one of those films that can be enjoyed for its whimsical silliness and the screwball performances by a cast who knew how to keep a straight face and their tongues in their cheeks.

Leading the proceedings with a seemingly endless series of double and triple takes is Cary Grant as Mortimer in a role that had been turned down by Bob Hope. When I was growing up, I was used to seeing an older, suave and relatively calm Cary Grant. The first time I saw *Arsenic and Old Lace,* I was amazed by his screwball antics and delivery. Perhaps he felt he needed to outdo the competition.

The old ladies were played by Josephine Hull – who literally bounced across the screen – and Jean Adair who, along with John Alexander as Teddy, had been in the original cast of the play and had their parts down pat. The evil Jonathan was played by Raymond Massey, made up to look like Boris Karloff (Karloff had been in the play) and the part of Dr. Einstein was taken by Peter Lorre who exhibited a genuine flair for comedy. Also along for the ride were stalwarts James Gleason, Jack Carson, and the inimitable Edward Everett Horton. It was all perfect casting, just about all of whom easily overshadowed poor Priscilla Lane as Grant's love interest.

Although there was a little bit of "opening up", it was obvious that this was a film based on a stage play and most of the action takes place in the large living room of the aunts' house. Not that this was a problem. Capra directed the action like a traffic cop knowing full well that the script and performers would carry the whole thing along. This was not typical Capra material. He had intended that the film would help to keep his family while he went away to war. But, although the movie was made in 1942, it was not released until 1944 because the play was still running on Broadway. There was a longstanding arrangement that films based on Broadway hits would not be released until after the play had finished its run. But the movie was worth waiting for.

The pace of the film seldom lets up, especially as Grant becomes increasingly frantic once he discovers what his kindly old aunts have been up to. He comments at one point that "insanity runs in my family – it practically gallops". The arrival of Massey and Lorre complicates things no end. But through it all, the two spinsters – and the marvelous Josephine Hull in particular – carry on as though murder was the most natural pastime in the world. This casual attitude towards homicide must have worried the censors at the time but not enough to put red lines through the script of an established hit except for the odd word or line of dialogue (most notably changing "I'm a bastard" to "I'm the son of a sea cook").

There is a charm and whimsy about *Arsenic and Old Lace* that comedies today do not possess. That charm is part of what makes the film so enjoyable and why it has stood up so well over the years – in addition to being very funny. When it was shown on television when I was a kid, all the boys in the neighborhood spent the next week running up staircases shouting "Charge!". I would still be tempted to do it except that stairs and I are not the best of friends these days.

Arsenic and Old Lace is one of those movies that is nice to take out every now and then for another enjoyable viewing. If we are lucky, there will never ever be a remake of it.

===============================

LAURA – 1944

A very stylish and even witty movie about obsession in which a detective slowly falls in love with the lovely victim of the alleged murder he is investigating. The audience is invited to do the same. As the title character, Gene Tierney is certainly beautiful enough to merit an obsession. She was a passable actress who really just needed to be there. The 1940s styles suited her which is not something that could be said of everyone.

Dana Andrews plays a slight variation on the typical *film noir* detective as he tries to unravel both the mystery and his emotions. Andrews is one of those actors who made a lot of movies but he is virtually forgotten today. An apparently intelligent actor in an age when smarts were not high on the list of requirements, *Laura* was one of his better films.

Stealing the film from both of them was eccentric character actor Clifton Webb as the waspish and self-absorbed writer Waldo Lydecker who also has reluctant feelings for Laura. This was Webb's first sound film and he went on to have a successful career playing snobs and supposed intellectuals. In *Laura,* he summed up his attitude by saying: "In my case, self-absorption is completely justified. I have never discovered any other subject quite so worthy of my attention." Webb gets some of the best lines in the picture and is one of those characters that audiences love to hate.

Also in the cast and giving it their all were Vincent Price and Judith Anderson. It is sometimes hard to remember that Price was a very effective actor in a number of movies before becoming the king of low budget horror. And Anderson was always in demand when a strong-minded older woman was required.

Laura was developed and directed by Otto Preminger who, along with Cecil B. DeMille was the last of the old-time movie directors who could be visualized wearing jodhpurs and shouting instructions through a megaphone. Preminger was not known for his deft touch which makes the success of *Laura* somewhat surprising. Despite his occasional successes, he was not a popular figure in the film community. Fellow director Billy Wilder said of him: "He's really Martin Bormann in elevator shoes with a facelift by a blindfolded plastic surgeon in Luxembourg." Preminger was famous for bullying actors and many who were the targets of his tirades swore never to work with him again. But he got results and in Hollywood that was what really counted.

Composer David Raskin contributed a memorable theme to *Laura* which, with lyrics added later by Johnny Mercer, quickly became a standard of the sort that is impossible to get out of your head. In the film, it helped to create an atmosphere that was a combination of romance and mystery that the audiences of the time apparently longed for. It is still quite effective today.

Above all, the film is a tribute to the radiance of Gene Tierney, a star who was never quite as big a star as she might have been. Her masculine first name was the result of being named after a favorite uncle. She was always recognized as a great beauty but she also suffered from manic depression, as well as a handicapped daughter, which eventually interfered with her work and resulted in her being put in a clinic for a short time. She made a couple of reasonably successful comebacks but finally decided to retire from acting. A well-publicized love life did not help matters. Luckily, she will be remembered for movies such as *Laura* more than anything else.

The famous portrait of Laura would later re-surface in other movies – in color. But *Laura* itself benefitted from being made in black and white. While the photography is not as striking as in, say, *Casablanca,* it is still much better suited to the material than color would have been. It is unfortunate that many people today feel negative towards black and white movies because many of them, as I hope this book illustrates, were genuine classics and not the outdated museum pieces that some consider them to be.

================================

THE BEST YEARS OF OUR LIVES – 1946

This was a totally absorbing postwar film which followed the fortunes of three servicemen attempting to re-adjust to civilian life in a society that seemed to take their experiences and sacrifices for granted. It was a kind of wake-up call to America and it made quite an impact, some of which can still be felt today. It is a long film – nearly three hours – but under the expert direction of William Wyler the time taken to tell the story hardly seems important.

The three servicemen, who share a memorable flight home, are soldier Fredric March, flyboy Dana Andrews, and sailor Harold Russell, a non-professional Canadian who had lost both hands in the war. They return to quite different lives but they continue to interact.

March is a successful banker who returns to a nice house and a loving wife played by Myrna Loy in a quietly effective straight role. Andrews had been a lowly soda jerk before the war and finds that wife Virginia Mayo has not really missed him all that much. The hardest reunion is between Russell and his girlfriend Cathy O'Donnell who have to come to terms with the hooks he now has in place of hands. Having won the war, the three servicemen now have to find a way to win, or at least survive, the peace.

Much of the success of *The Best Years of Our Lives* is due to the outstanding cast and their ability to arouse the right mixture of emotion and anger in the audience. Fredric March is as hammy an actor as ever but manages to get away with it. Dana Andrews is solid and sympathetic in the face of adversity. But it is Harold Russell who makes the biggest impression, making light of his predicament with the guys but falling apart when facing the reality of the future. Russell was the first non-professional to win an Oscar. In fact, he won two for this picture – a special award and the one for best supporting actor. The film also won for best picture, best actor (March), best screenplay (Robert E. Sherwood), and best director. Producer Sam Goldwyn famously said: "I don't care if it doesn't make a nickel. I just want every man, woman and child in America to see it."

The film was successful in pricking the collective American conscience – an indication of just how influential a movie could be, at least in those days. It surprised everybody by being the top box office draw that year and became an inspiration for later film makers. A kind of remake was done in the 1970s called *Returning Home* which presented the same situation but in relation to the Vietnam War.

As with any classic film, *The Best Years of Our Lives* has its memorable moments. One was when soda jerk Andrews punches a customer for telling Russell that his sacrifice had been in vain. Another was March's impassioned speech at the end of the movie. But the most poignant scene was between Russell and his fiancée Cathy O'Donnell in which he forces her to help him remove his prosthetic arms to show her what their nightly ritual would be if she decides to go ahead with their marriage.

William Wyler was always a skillful director who was noted for being good with actors. He also had a great deal of empathy with these characters having been in the war himself and suffering permanent hearing damage while flying in a B-17 bomber. *The Best Years of Our Lives* was his first film after returning to Hollywood from the war and he probably required a bit of re-adjustment himself. Supposedly, the scene in which March and Loy are reunited is based on Wyler's own reunion with his wife.

After years of patriotic war films and frothy escapist fare, a more or less realistic drama must have made a nice change of pace for movie audiences in the immediate postwar days. Everyone probably longed to get back to a normal life which is what *The Best Years of Our Lives* was all about. It was also the time that saw the creation of the Baby Boomers – my generation – that would tend to look at things somewhat differently. We all grew up with fathers who had been in the war and a movie like *The Best Years of Our Lives* gave us some insight into what they had been through. It may seem like ancient history now but films like this assure they will never be totally forgotten.

===============================

THE THIRD MAN – 1949

I once read a review of *The Third Man* that claimed it was "a perfect movie". It is hardly that but it is a pretty good flick, once you get into the mood of it and are able to tune out the zither music of Anton Karas. As far as I am concerned, a little zither music goes a long way and *The Third Man* theme in particular soon threatens to become annoying rather than evocative.

The Third Man was a collaboration between director Carol Reed and writer Graham Greene. They had worked successfully before and wanted to do another film together but were stuck for an idea until Greene came up with a suitable premise. Some of Greene's books did not necessarily transfer well to the screen but because *The Third Man* was envisaged as a film it seemed to work and gave Reed plenty of scope to bring it to life.

The movie was set in postwar Vienna and was partly filmed there at a time when shooting on location was still something of a novelty. The setting added greatly to the atmosphere which was further helped by some suitably stark black and white photography. The basic story involved the search by Joseph Cotten for an old friend – the elusive Harry Lime – unaware that his friend had changed since the good old days and that the authorities, led by the very stuffy Trevor Howard, would also like to locate him. Along the way he encounters a sultry female in the form of Italian actress Alida Valli. Once Cotten finds Lime, in the shape of Orson Welles, things begin to heat up considerably.

Because of the talent involved, *The Third Man* could easily be regarded as a British film. As it turned out, two versions were released – an American one with narration by Cotten and a slightly longer British one that was narrated by director Reed.

It is hard to imagine that the bland Joseph Cotten was the first choice to play the oddly named Holly Martins. He was hardly the sort of actor that audiences could care about very much. It was said that the only reason he became a leading man was that he was tall, reasonably good looking, had curly hair and was useless at character parts. Somehow, his blandness seems to work in his favor in *The Third Man* but how he attained stardom in the first place remains a mystery. Apparently, he could mix quite wicked martinis.

I have always been somewhat mystified by the reverence that so many people give to Orson Welles, but then I never thought *Citizen Kane* was all that great. He was an actor, writer, producer and director who was always struggling to make the movies he wanted. To finance his projects, he worked for other people. Any success he had seemed to be due to the force of his personality. He was known as the oldest *enfant terrible* in the world. The wit Dorothy Parker said that meeting Welles was like meeting God without dying. And glamorous Rita Hayworth explained that she divorced Welles because she could not take his genius anymore.

When film fanatics think of *The Third Man,* the first image that comes into their minds is Welles's initial appearance when, standing in darkness, he is suddenly illuminated by the light of a nearby window. It is a memorable image. It is not difficult to forget about Joseph Cotten or anyone else when Welles is on the screen. He seems to raise the whole tone of the movie. It is interesting to note that the original choice to play Harry Lime had been Noël Coward.

Still, Welles is only on the screen for a relatively brief time. The rest of the movie belongs to Cotten, Howard and the sensuous Alida Valli. And Welles was nowhere in sight when Cotten and Valli shared that very memorable final scene, a scene that caused much debate among the film makers. Keeping it was, of course, the right decision but it was a strange way to end a movie in 1949.

The Third Man was both a critical and commercial success when it was released in both Britain and the USA and has gone on to be regarded as something of a masterpiece by people who are not shy about using that word to describe a movie. No less a film critic than Roger Ebert lists it among his favorite films as well as citing Harry Lime as his favorite screen villain. It is, of course, an extremely well-made *film noir* full of dark shadows and crazy angles. I only wish it had a better leading man and much less zither music.

================================

ALL ABOUT EVE – 1950

"Fasten your seat belts. We're in for a bumpy night." – one of the more memorable lines in a movie filled with crackling dialogue and even more crackling performances. *All About Eve* tells the story of a very ambitious young actress who worms her way into the inner circle of an established and very temperamental star and proceeds to use everyone in her quest for stardom. It is one of the bitchiest films ever made and all the more enjoyable for it because the bitchiness is delivered and displayed with such wit and style. Writer and director Joseph L. Mankiewicz gives his cast everything they need to light up the screen and they do not disappoint. As a backstage story, it is enough to make anyone think twice about becoming an actor.

The movie marked a return to form for the great Bette Davis whom many had considered washed up. She dominates the film as Margo Channing, as well she might. The role seems tailor made for her although it was originally intended for Claudette Colbert. There has been much speculation about who Davis's character was based on but it would appear that Bette's performance was a thinly disguised portrait of her old rival Tallulah Bankhead who was understandably not pleased.

Matching Davis in the acting stakes was Anne Baxter as the titular Eve in a nicely calculated performance that subtly captures the moods of the would-be usurper. Baxter suits the part being striking rather than beautiful with fire often flashing in her scheming eyes.

Not content with having two superb leads, Mankiewicz populates his script with an assortment of characters who all make impressive contributions to the proceedings. Chief among them is the very droll George Sanders as an acid-tongued critic (is there any other kind?), Gary Merrill (who Davis would fall in love with and marry) as a no-nonsense theatre director, Hugh Marlowe as a somewhat neurotic playwright (again, is there any other kind?), Celeste Holm as Marlowe's wife who, for a supporting player, gets some very juicy lines, and pint-sized but formidable Thelma Ritter in her usual role as a wise-cracking maid. There was even a small but very showy part for young Marilyn Monroe in one of her early films.

If *All About Eve* has a flaw, it is its running time of well over two hours which produces a couple of dull patches. But these soon pass and the fur and feathers begin to fly once again. The action may shift from place to place but the attitudes remain intact as Mankiewicz directs traffic in a single direction – upwards for Eve.

The film had a suitably stylish look especially with the costumes designed for Bette Davis by the legendary Edith Head. In her long career, Head dressed virtually every female star in Hollywood and collected multiple Academy Awards for doing so. Far from being a great beauty herself, it was rumored that she was gay, especially when she occasionally bragged that she had seen all of Hollywood's most beautiful women naked. One of my favorite bits of show business graffiti was glimpsed backstage at a theatre and read: "Edith Head gives good costume."

When Oscar time rolled around, *All About Eve* received a record fourteen nominations including two for best actress (Davis and Baxter lost out to Judy Holliday for *Born Yesterday*). It did take the award for best picture as well as Best Supporting Actor for George Sanders and two awards for Mankiewicz for best screenplay and best director – all of which were richly deserved.

Despite not winning the Oscar, *All About Eve* was a triumph for Bette Davis because, at age 42, it revived her faltering career and led the way to more starring roles, some better than others. She proved she could be versatile and not just the star of "weepies". Claudette Colbert told her: "You're the luckiest of us all. You started playing older women when you were young so you never had to bridge the gap." I think that was intended as a compliment.

All About Eve was cynical as well as stylish and witty. It marked the beginning of change in movies during the Fifties when film makers still gave audiences credit for some intelligence. It was a movie that you had to listen to. It was also a cinema experience to be savored.

================================

SUNSET BOULEVARD – 1950

1950 was apparently a vintage year for cynicism. Few film makers could match the droll cynicism of Billy Wilder on a movie like *Sunset Boulevard.* Working from a script that he co-wrote with Charles Brackett, director Wilder treats the audience to a less than flattering behind the scenes view of Hollywood in his tale of a desperate screen writer's weird involvement with an eccentric and somewhat unhinged old silent movie star planning her comeback.

The film has a memorable opening as the camera discovers a body floating face down in the swimming pool of a posh but slightly faded Los Angeles mansion. The story is then told in flashback, narrated by the dead body in the pool. If this seems somewhat strange, consider the picture's original opening scene that was set in a morgue and featured corpses sitting up and discussing how they died with one another. Wilder's imagination was running a tad on overdrive on *Sunset Boulevard* and the audience was the lucky beneficiary.

The writer was played by very masculine William Holden who was a very busy actor in the early Fifties. His good looks and gruff voice seemed to suit the era although he was not everyone's cup of tea. He is, of course, the body in the pool and the story of how he ended up there is by turns weird, comic and nostalgic for the age of silent pictures.

As the one-time silent screen goddess Norma Desmond, the great Gloria Swanson returns to the screen in a fascinating performance of ego and self-delusion. She was only 52 at the time *Sunset Boulevard* was made but back in those days 52 was considered to be much older than it is today. She dominates proceedings like a true star, reveling in the glory of her past and convinced her public is impatient for her return. When Holden comments that she used to be big in pictures, Swanson instantly replies: "I *am* big. It's the pictures that got small." She basks in the glow of her silent movies. "We didn't need dialogue," she says. "We had faces then." It is not difficult for the audience to become trapped in Swanson's world that way Holden is.

Back around 1970, I happened to see Gloria Swanson on the Dick Cavett show on which the other guest was a bemused Janis Joplin. The interaction and mutual respect between these two very individualistic women from two totally different eras was amazing. Swanson was a feisty old bird and still strangely attractive.

In the role of Swanson's butler/chauffer/companion was another relic from the silent era, Erich von Stroheim, a legendary director famous for his excesses both on screen and off. He was also an actor, usually portraying sneering German military types who many considered to be little more than a parody of his own personality. Clips from his uncompleted film *Queen Kelly* that starred Gloria Swanson were used in *Sunset Boulevard* to illustrate Norma Desmond's silent career. Other silent stars such as Buster Keaton and H.B. Warner also put in an appearance as well as Cecil B. DeMille in a cameo portraying himself.

It must remembered that sound pictures had only been around for a little over twenty years when *Sunset Boulevard* was made and Hollywood was still full of veterans from the silent era, some faring better than others and all of them nostalgic for the good old days.

Not everyone in Hollywood appreciated Wilder's view of the film industry and there was a certain degree of secrecy when *Sunset Boulevard* was being filmed to keep the storyline from leaking out too soon. When the film was released, MGM's Louis B. Mayer took particular offense to it and declared that Wilder should be tarred and feathered and run out of town. Fortunately, critics and audiences felt differently and when *Sunset Boulevard* played at Radio City Music Hall in New York, the line for tickets was three blocks long.

Despite her personal success in the film, Gloria Swanson did not make many films after *Sunset Boulevard* and finished her career by playing herself in the dire *Airport 75*. With the exception of *Sunset Boulevard,* she will be primarily remembered for her silent films and her best-selling autobiography.

Films like *Sunset Boulevard* and *All About Eve* revealed that show business was not all fun and glamour. They also helped pave the way for a more realistic – and, yes, some would say cynical – look at life. But even more important, movies like this were fascinating to experience.

===================================

HARVEY – 1950

James Stewart, popular Hollywood leading man and World War Two bomber pilot, had his career take a slightly strange turn in 1950 when he starred in *Harvey,* a whimsical tale about a lovable lush whose best friend was a six foot tall rabbit that no one else could see. The film was based on a very successful Broadway play whose author, Mary Chase, also worked on the screenplay which tried hard to disguise its theatrical origins. The movie was directed by veteran Henry Koster who was not particularly known for doing comedies but the material and cast were so good that he could hardly go wrong.

Stewart, as Elwood P. Dowd, ambles through the film in his usual lanky, good-natured way, unaware of the chaos that he is causing around him, in particular to his harassed socially ambitious sister, played with perfection by Oscar winner Josephine Hull who had performed the role on stage and, in many ways, became the driving force of the plot as she struggles to control her well-meaning brother and his usual pal. This eventually involves the staff at a local and, apparently, not that good asylum.

Like *Arsenic and Old Lace* before it, *Harvey* tends to treat things like mental illness and alcoholism like amusing eccentricities rather than serious problems. Stewart spends a lot of time drinking and in bars but he is never anything less than genial, saying nice things to a pretty girl and inviting strangers home for dinner. The audience is never allowed to worry about Stewart's condition, only that he might be cured. In this regard, it is not just Elwood P. Dowd who is living in a rather nice fantasy world.

Josephine Hull's anxiety over the effects of her brother's behavior on her naïve daughter's social chances - "Myrtle Mae, you have a lot to learn and I hope you never learn it" – leads her to taking Stewart to the asylum where, because this is a bit of a farce, nothing goes according to plan.

The asylum is staffed by people who might have been stock characters if it were not for the quality of the script. Cecil Kellaway is the somewhat befuddled head doctor, handsome Charles Drake is his capable assistant, Peggy Dow is the pretty receptionist with eyes on Drake, and veteran Jesse White plays a no-nonsense orderly who takes a fancy to Hull's gawky daughter Victoria Horne. At this point, the movie becomes almost an ensemble piece with Stewart floating nonchalantly through it all. And somewhere there is an invisible six foot rabbit – a pooka – who is the cause of it all.

Harvey is what might be termed a gentle comedy. There are a couple of laugh out loud moments but it mostly produces chuckles and permanent smiles. It is amusing rather than hilarious but no less enjoyable for that. The cast works well together and James Stewart seems to be having the time of his life. He seems to relish delivering lines such as "I've wrestled with reality for thirty-five years and I'm happy to state I finally won out over it."

Needless to say, *Harvey* was a very popular film and continues to find new audiences today. James Stewart picked up an Oscar nomination but it was Josephine Hull who got the well-deserved award as best supporting actress for what was arguably the most difficult role on the movie. There have been several remakes – including one with Stewart in the 1970s – as well as countless revivals of the stage play, both professional and amateur, but it is the 1950 version that is the best.

I've often thought that *Harvey* would make a great double bill with *Arsenic and Old Lace* (they both share Josephine Hull). They are a pair of genuinely whimsical pictures whose charm could never be duplicated today. And both films demonstrate what a rich supply of talented character actors existed in the old studio days which, despite their flaws, produced so many great movies. It is a tad ironic that James Stewart at the time he made *Harvey* started a trend that eventually contributed to the downfall of the studio system. He opted to take a percentage of the picture's profits rather than a straight salary, an example that was soon followed by many others.

Harvey the pooka may or may not exist. But *Harvey* the movie is there for everyone to see and enjoy.

==============================

BORN YESTERDAY – 1950

Another Broadway success to come to the big screen in 1950 was *Born Yesterday* with its original star, the wonderfully inimitable Judy Holliday. Columbia's Harry Cohn had resisted having Holliday in the film but her success in the stage version and in a supporting role in the Tracy/Hepburn film *Adam's Rib* made her casting inevitable. As a result, she not only preserved her magnificent stage performance on celluloid but she ended up with the Oscar for best actress, beating the likes of Bette Davis and Gloria Swanson.

Judy Holliday made a career out of playing dumb blondes but she was actually a very intelligent woman with a high IQ. She was able to give her dumb blondes depth and vulnerability – a talent she shared with Marilyn Monroe. She only made a handful of films before succumbing to cancer in 1965 at the age of 43 but those movies were memorable and *Born Yesterday* was the best of them all.

My favorite Judy Holliday story involves her being chased around the desk of the odious Harry Cohn in his office. She finally stopped, pulled the falsies out of her brassiere and handed them to Cohn saying: "I think these are what you're after."

Garson Kanin wrote the play of *Born Yesterday* and also wrote the screenplay although he did not receive credit for it. He also had a bad history with Harry Cohn and it was no secret that the part of the uncouth and slovenly tycoon played by Broderick Crawford was based on Cohn. A million dollars being paid for the film rights to a play will create strange bedfellows.

Crawford played a less than scrupulous businessman who comes to Washington to bribe or otherwise influence a Congressman or two in his favor. With him is his ex-showgirl mistress Billie Dawn who in unforgettably portrayed by Judy Holliday. After a disastrous social meeting, Crawford decides that Holliday needs some polish and education and hires cynical writer William Holden to tutor her in the finer things in life. This modern take on *Pygmalion* provides some of the movie's more amusing moments but also allows for a postwar re-examination of American values. Crawford soon discovers that where someone like his mistress is concerned, a little education can be a dangerous thing.

Holliday, of course, takes a shine to Holden and he eventually realizes how irresistible she can be in addition to being the key to his writing a damning exposé of Crawford. The interplay between the three main characters is fascinating and superbly acted by all concerned. But the common denominator in everything is the sparkling Judy Holliday who delivers juicy lines in a voice that has to be heard to be believed.

Broderick Crawford had recently won the Oscar for best actor for *All the King's Men* and clearly enjoyed playing slightly larger than life unsympathetic characters. William Holden, meanwhile, was basically William Holden although he probably smiled more in *Born Yesterday* than in most of his other films. There was also a notable supporting role for Howard St. John as Crawford's oily lawyer with questionable values. But every scene was easily stolen by Judy Holliday.

The very experienced director George Cukor, known for his rapport with actresses, approached the project with a healthy respect for its stage origins. He even arranged theater-style rehearsals for the cast before filming to perfect the rhythm of the piece. He also managed to move some scenes away from the single set of the original and took advantage of some location shots of Washington although some of these look like back projections of second unit work. But he did not allow anything to interfere with the characters and dialogue which were the heart of the movie. It was soon apparent to everyone – with the possible exception of Harry Cohn – that Judy Holliday was a force to be reckoned with.

There are some wonderful individual moments in *Born Yesterday.* The scene in which Holliday constantly beats Crawford at gin rummy is worth the price of admission on its own. And no one can shout "What?" the way Holliday could. Even the way she moved was amazing. The picture may get a tad preachy towards the end but this can be forgiven by all the magic that has gone before. The movie is occasionally dramatic but it is mostly a very funny comedy with one of cinema's finest comediennes in firm control. Aspects of *Born Yesterday* may have dated somewhat but not its humor.

==================================

THE LAVENDER HILL MOB – 1951

In the postwar years, British films found a measure of popularity in America largely due to a series of rather whimsical comedies from Ealing Studios, many of which featured Alec Guinness. One of the very best of these was *The Lavender Hill Mob,* a heist film unlike any other.

Guinness played a mild-mannered and slightly eccentric clerk in the Bank of England whose duties included overseeing the transfer of gold bullion to the bank. For years he had dreamed of stealing the vanload of gold bars but realized that such a theft was pointless unless there was a way of getting the gold out of the country. A solution presented itself when Stanley Holloway moved into the same boarding house as Guinness. Holloway owned a small foundry that made souvenirs of famous places around the world. Watching the workers produce some lead paperweights of the Eiffel Tower, Guinness has a flash of inspiration and confides his plan to Holloway who is more than willing to cooperate.

To help carry out the heist, the conspirators enlist the help of two professional criminals played by a pair of Britain's most reliable character actors, Sidney James and Alfie Bass. With the "mob" complete, the job goes ahead, more or less according to plan, and they make off with a million pounds in gold – quite a considerable sum in those days.

Script writer T.E.B. Clarke, a veteran of crime films, was uncertain about how the robbery could be credibly pulled off so he asked the Bank of England for advice. Amazingly, the Bank put together a committee to study the question and came up with a plan – the plan that was used in the film. It is difficult to imagine such a lapse in security happening today.

The film was directed by Charles Crichton who took advantage of the London locations which greatly helped the look of the picture. In fact, *The Lavender Hill Mob* provides an interesting view of London at that time in which the damage of World War Two was still visible in places. Very little of London still looks the same now. And it is amazing and slightly amusing to see speeding police cars ringing bells instead of having sirens.

Amusing is a very appropriate word for *The Lavender Hill Mob* as it is the sort of quaint British comedy that produces mild chuckles rather than belly laughs. That does not make it any less entertaining as it packs quite a lot into its relatively brief running time. It was unfortunate that the moral code of the time did not allow crime to pay.

Guinness and Holloway are marvelous in the lead roles and bounce off one another like a seasoned comedy team. Guinness was best known at that time for starring in these sorts of droll Ealing comedies – his more serious roles in the likes of *The Bridge of the River Kwai* and *Tinker, Tailor, Soldier, Spy* – not forgetting *Star Wars* – were still in his future. Guinness was apparently as strange off-screen as he was on. He once said of himself: "I don't really know who I am – quite possibly I don't exist at all."

Stanley Holloway was not quite such a film star but would soon play his most famous role as Eliza Dolittle's father in *My Fair Lady* on both stage and screen.

The film is populated by the usual solid cast of British supporting players such as John Gregson and Sidney Tafler with special mention going to Edie Martin as Guinness and Holloway's fussy landlady who chides them for being "naughty men". As an extra treat, a very young Audrey Hepburn is seen briefly near the beginning of the picture in what is possibly her first film role.

One of the most memorable scenes in the movie involved Guinness and Holloway running down a circular service stairway on the Eiffel Tower. The constant swirling movement and quick editing produced a dizzying feeling of vertigo, especially when intercut with shots of the ground below. It was an unusual sequence for a comedy film which looked remarkable on the big screen. I was lucky enough to see the movie when it was reissued in the early Sixties and those images have always stayed with me.

The Lavender Hill Mob was popular with both critics and audiences and has held up quite well. It received an Oscar for its clever screenplay and a best actor nomination for Guinness. With or without awards, it remains a very delightful film.

===================================

MONSIEUR HULOT'S HOLIDAY – 1953

One of the more unusual films in this compendium is the French movie *Monsieur Hulot's Holiday* or, to give it its proper title *Les Vacances de Monsieur Hulot,* a delightful throwback to the spirit of silent comedies. This was a film by talented Jacques Tati who wrote, directed and starred in it as a character he would go on to play in several more equally off-the-wall pictures. Here Hulot was established as a basically well-meaning, extremely courteous but terminally klutzy individual with an amazing capacity for creating havoc wherever he went, often without even noticing it.

There is very little plot to *Monsieur Hulot's Holiday.* It is basically a series of episodes and gags that occur during Hulot's stay at a small and relatively unspoiled seaside town on the Brittany coast. Hulot interacts with the staff at his hotel and with some of the other holidaymakers, some of whom were actual tourists drafted into the film. It is a nostalgic snapshot of the sort of French beach holidays that are no longer possible.

Jacques Tati was an accomplished mime with an extensive background in French music hall. Dialogue in the film is kept to a complete minimum with most of it coming from characters other than Hulot. But this is hardly a silent movie. Tati loved sound and used it to great effect in his films such as the repetitive (and amplified) squeak of a swinging door. This combination of visual humor with sound effects and music (by Alain Romans) give the film its unique sense of charm.

The picture and the humor in it is very French. This is not a bad thing but it may take some getting used to. In France, the image of the gangling Hulot with his hat and pipe and uncertain walk would become as much an icon as Chaplin's little tramp. He would also become an inspiration, not just for comic actors but also for other film makers. François Truffaut was a great admirer of Tati's visual style and even included a brief homage to the Hulot character in *Domicile Conjugal (Bed and Board)*.

Tati enjoyed using amateurs in his films for the naturalness they brought with them. In *Monsieur Hulot's Holiday*, this included the charming Nathalie Pascaud who captivated audiences but sadly decided that a life in the movies was not for her. Perhaps because the film was so different and had so little dialogue, it proved popular in many other countries and even garnered an Oscar nomination for its screenplay. Sometimes the relaxed attitude of the picture make it hard to believe that it actually had a screenplay but that it just another indication of Tati's artistry. Even when it looks like nothing is happening, something is going on.

There are a number of quite funny set pieces including Hulot's attempts to play tennis or his inability to propel a kayak. Even Hulot's old 1920s banger of a car is a source of amusement. Like all great comics, especially the ones from the silent era, Hulot does not have a very good working relationship with inanimate objects. But he is seldom discouraged. Setbacks are brushed off and he simply moves on to the next thing.

Monsieur Hulot's Holiday was filmed in the little town of Saint-Marc-sur-Mer in the days before mass tourism became such an industry in European coastal locales. My wife and her family had been taking continental holidays since she was a girl and the setting for *Monsieur Hulot's Holiday* brought back many memories for her of what places along France's Atlantic coast used to be like. The town has probably changed somewhat but the connection with Tati has never been forgotten. A bronze statue of Monsieur Hulot now overlooks the seafront. The Hôtel de la Plage where the character of Hulot stayed – as well as the cast and film crew – is still open for business.

Jacques Tati was, above all, a shrewd observer of human behavior and folly. But he never laughed at people or judged them – unless they deserved it. His films were gems of looking at life with constant amusement and occasional exasperation. Films like *Monsieur Hulot's Holiday* and *Mon Oncle* with their scant dialogue and even less plot are cinema classics in anybody's book. I can remember a time when people used to say that the French regarded Jerry Lewis as a comic genius. I find that hard to believe when the French had their very own comic genius in Jacques Tati.

===================================

ON THE WATERFRONT – 1954

On the Waterfront was a powerful film when it was released in 1954. It still possesses a bit of a punch today but modern audiences tend to view it more with curiosity than emotion. It contains what is probably the best screen performance by Marlon Brando whose style was still new and exciting in those days without the touches of excess that marred his later career. And its story of a longshoreman who turns stool pigeon against a very corrupt union was seen by some as an apology or even justification by director Elia Kazan and writer Budd Schulberg for having testified at the McCarthy witch hunt hearings that were such an embarrassment and disgrace in American political history. *On the Waterfront* was a deadly serious film that dealt with organized crime in a way the old gangster movies never did. It also found time for some fairly moving examination of human feelings and relationships.

Despite everything else, it is Brando's performance that draws us into the film and keeps us there. Not everyone was a fan of his method approach to acting. Some considered him to be little more than a mumbling hooligan who, as one critic put it, "sounds like he has a mouth full of wet toilet paper." But many found the Brando style to be refreshingly modern and few could deny the impact he had made in *A Streetcar Named Desire* which he played on both stage and screen. He was, in the 1950s, the biggest thing to hit movies since the arrival of sound. Brando was so perfect for the role of Terry Malloy that it is difficult to comprehend that Frank Sinatra was considered for the part at one point.

But Brando was not the whole film. Kazan surrounded him with a supporting cast of actors who were more than capable of holding their own against him. This was perhaps best illustrated in the famous "I coulda been a contender" taxicab scene between Brando and Rod Steiger. At this point in his career, Steiger was still a pretty good actor before he became a notorious over-actor. Chewing of the scenery in *On the Waterfront* was left to Lee J. Cobb as the seedy union boss. Cobb was an actor they frequently turned to when a bombastic performance was required. Somewhere in the middle, in the part of a conscience-stricken priest, was Karl Malden, an actor who could play the role of Cyrano de Bergerac with no additional makeup.

A love interest for Brando was provided by Eva Marie Saint in, I think, her film debut. She played the convent-educated daughter of a fellow longshoreman whose brother was a victim of the murderous union boss. She managed to be lovely and touching while appearing plain and unglamorous. Her scenes with Brando provide an entirely different kind of emotion to the film. She probably had to work hard at those scenes. Many of Brando's co-stars through the years complained at how he never seemed to "be there" and was not a giver. Steiger complained that while shooting the taxicab scene, when it came time to do the close-ups, Steiger stayed on the set to feed Brando his lines but when it was time for Steiger's close-ups, Brando walked off and left Steiger to do his lines with an assistant director.

Helping everything along was an outstanding musical score by classical composer and conductor Leonard Bernstein. The music for *On the Waterfront* was not a typical movie soundtrack in the same way that his music for *West Side Story* would not be a typical Broadway score. Bernstein's soaring main theme and some of his incidental music perfectly matched Kazan's hard-hitting images. At the same time, he provided a jazzy love theme that caught the mood of the times.

Whatever its philosophies or political implications, *On the Waterfront* remains a powerful film with much of the credit due to the single-minded vision of Elia Kazan. The fact that he never made another film as good or as important was probably due to his personality more than his talent. It was said that he lacked basic social graces and, what is more, did not care. Vivien Leigh, the Oscar-winning star of his previous success *A Streetcar Named Desire* said he was "the kind of man who sends a suit out to be cleaned and rumpled."

When Oscar time came, *On the Waterfront* picked up eight awards including those for best picture, actor, director, screenplay and supporting actress. It seemed an odd film to be such a popular success. Today it is probably only watched for Brando's performance.

===============================

THE SMALLEST SHOW ON EARTH – 1957

While it may not be described as a classic film in the usual sense, *The Smallest Show on Earth* is a movie that I have a lot of affection for and for that reason it is included in this book. It is one of those charming and gentle British comedies that were made by the dozen during the Fifties and early Sixties except that a few, like this one, had something special about them. The movie tells the story of a young couple who inherit a cinema in a small town only to discover that it is little better than a ruin staffed by a trio of geriatric eccentrics. They decide to try to bring the theater back to life with the usual mixed results.

Experienced director Basil Dearden handles everything in a relatively straightforward manner, giving his talented cast plenty of space and opportunity to shine.

The leading roles were taken by real-life couple sturdy Bill Travers and demure Virginia McKenna. Travers had had some minor successes in films without ever really making an impression. He spends most of *The Smallest Show on Earth* being either confused or exasperated and in need of calming down by his wife. McKenna, on the other hand, is an oasis of calm who is more bemused than worried by the various obstacles and disasters that they encounter. McKenna was actually a more recognized star than her husband but they worked very well together. Both seemed to realize that, whatever they did, they were going to be upstaged by their supporting cast.

The inherited and rather ancient staff at the Bijou consisted of alcoholic projectionist Peter Sellers who seemed to like playing old men at this time, the ever imposing Margaret Rutherford as the no-nonsense box office cashier with the wonderful name of Mrs. Fazackalee, and Bernard Miles as the slow-witted and slow-moving doorman whose dream was to have a proper uniform.

The Smallest Show on Earth was made at a time when Peter Sellers was still basically a comic character actor. He easily made the transition from radio's *Goon Show* to the movies with his knack for voices and accents and his love of heavy makeup. His film career was just taking off and he would make many memorable comedies before international stardom spoiled him and he became simply a clown. Margaret Rutherford was a perfect foil for him and always able to hold her own against him.

Helping the couple out was Leslie Phillips in an early role. He went on to play many suave ladies' men with questionable motives but here he played a very rare creature indeed - a sympathetic lawyer.

Even in 1957, *The Smallest Show on Earth* was a film tinged with nostalgia. There is a marvelous scene where Travers and McKenna returned after a night out (they lived in a dilapidated flat above the theater) to find an after-hours performance going on of a silent film being run just for the staff with Mrs. Fazackalee providing the musical accompaniment on piano. It is a quietly touching moment that makes a nice counterpoint to the chaos that had gone before such as Sellers' ongoing battle with his own equipment, especially when trains were coming and going into the nearby station.

Set in the fictional northern town of Sloughborough, most of the location work was actually done in and around London. The Britain portrayed in the film barely exists anymore which makes the movie seem almost like a fantasy today. *The Smallest Show on Earth,* like the Bijou itself, had modest ambitions and, for the most part, achieved them. It is an extremely enjoyable film. There is a somewhat strange aspect to the ending, however, in that it suggests that sometimes crime can pay which was a sentiment that was rarely allowed to be expressed in a picture in those days.

The film was sometimes known as *Big Time Operators* in America which is another example of British irony. It is a nice film about little people struggling against the world and occasionally coming out on top. The movie is a must for fans of Margaret Rutherford and the early work of Peter Sellers. Some viewers might also be interested to see what Travers and McKenna were up to prior to *Born Free.* As they say in Britain, *The Smallest Show on Earth* does exactly what it says on the tin – it delivers a pleasant and amusing little movie that is well worth seeing more than once.

=================================

WITNESS FOR THE PROSECUTION – 1957

It was an irresistible combination – Billy Wilder using his magic touch to direct a clever Agatha Christie courtroom drama featuring a trio of stars who were all slightly past their peak but enjoying themselves immensely. *Witness for the Prosecution* had been a success on stage and Wilder and Harry Kurnitz expertly adapted it for the screen with minimal effort to disguise its theatrical origin. The film is neatly divided into two acts – the first set in the chambers of wily barrister Sir Wilfrid Robarts where the basic plot and characters are introduced with a mild flourish and the second act in an Old Bailey courtroom where everything begins to hot up.

The murder case that propels the plot at times seems almost incidental to the movie. Evidence is discussed in great detail but it is the way it is done that fascinates. There is some subtlety in the presentation but it is not overly subtle. This is because of the performances of the stars.

Tyrone Power got top billing and the least flashy part as the bewildered defendant who is not all that he seems. The incredibly handsome Power was an established leading man who had appeared in swashbucklers, musicals and dramas in which his straightforward and seemingly earnest performances threatened to appear wooden. In *Witness for the Prosecution,* he managed to appear somewhat seedy which suited the role of someone accused of murdering an old lady for her money. As it turned out, this was his last completed film. He died of a heart attack in 1958 at the age of 44 on the set of *Solomon and Sheba.*

Playing Power's foreign-born wife was the indomitable and always somewhat mannish Marlene Dietrich with an edge that was not always present in her performances. She added much of the mystery to the proceedings and to satisfy fans of her famous legs, a flashback was created to showcase her musical talents which were, it must be said, minimal. But she was excellent in the rest of the movie and fully expected to receive an Oscar nomination for it. She was reportedly quite upset when she did not.

For me, the best reason to see *Witness for the Prosecution* was the carefully calculated but deliciously hammy performance of Charles Laughton as Sir Wilfrid, the cunning barrister. As an actor, Laughton was unique and improved a number of movies simply by being in them. He had, by his own admission, a face that could stop a sundial but he had a powerful presence that few could control. Alfred Hitchcock remarked: "You can't direct a Laughton picture. The best you can hope for is to referee." Wilder seems to have taken this advice and allows Laughton to dominate every scene he is in, although he gets some competition from his co-stars.

The supporting cast includes Laughton's real life wife Elsa Lanchester as his dictator of a nurse and reliable character actors such as Henry Daniell, John Williams, Una O'Connor, and Torin Thatcher in small but pivotal parts.

Although *Witness for the Prosecution* looks for all the world like a British film, it was actually an American production that was mostly filmed in Hollywood where the Old Bailey courtroom was painstakingly recreated. My English wife who, for reasons we will not go into, was once a witness in an Old Bailey trial told me how accurate and intimidating the set was.

Billy Wilder directs everything with a very sure touch and, with the exception of the unnecessary flashback, keeps the plot humming along with equal dashes of mystery and humor. In fact, it is the fairly witty humor that raises *Witness for the Prosecution* above most other courtroom dramas. Agatha Christie announced that she was pleased with the result and that the movie was the first decent film that had been made from one of her stories.

Witness for the Prosecution was nominated for a number of Academy Awards but did not win any of them. This did not diminish its popularity. There have been several remakes, mostly for television, including one starring the great Ralph Richardson in the 1980s and a much more recent BBC mini-series in which the characters and plot were altered somewhat. There are also rumors of another movie version in the pipeline but I personally cannot see the point of making *Witness for the Prosecution* without Charles Laughton.

==================================

THE 400 BLOWS – 1959

One of my all-time favorite film makers was the French director François Truffaut. *The 400 Blows* (*Les Quatre Cents Coups*) was his first feature film which helped to launch the French "new wave" or *nouvelle vague*. Truffaut had previously been a critic with very strong views for *Cahiers du Cinema* where he developed a belief in the *auteur* theory that the director was the true author of a motion picture. In *The 400 Blows* he was able to test that theory.

The fairly episodic plot follows the misadventures of a thirteen year old Parisian delinquent named Antoine Doinel who has more imagination than common sense. Most of what Antoine does is based on incidents in Truffaut's early life and is related with candor rather than any sense of nostalgia for a lost or misspent youth. Antoine has faults but he is determined to be his own person.

The casting of Antoine Doinel was crucial and fate was very kind to Truffaut in providing his perfect alter ego in the form of young Jean-Pierre Léaud who displayed a natural talent with no fear of the camera. It is the partnership and bond between Truffaut and Léaud that gives the movie its strength and heart and the young actor, despite the faults of his character, easily engages the emotions of the audience as he rebels against authority in virtually every form. The French expression *faire les quatre cents coups* has no easy translation into English – it is a phrase that more or less means to raise hell or kick against authority. Antoine does both.

The Paris locations and almost documentary-style camerawork gives the film its distinctive look. The story is by turns humorous and brutal but Truffaut seemed determined that it not be sad. Instead, it was honest or, at least, as honest as he was prepared to be. He said later, perhaps a little teasingly, "I am much less autobiographical than people think." But people who knew him well felt that Antoine could just as easily have been named François.

The 400 Blows and its final freeze frame shot were a big hit at the Cannes Film Festival where Truffaut was named best director at the age of 27. This led to the film finding international success on the art house circuit which helped to pave the way for movies by other New Wave directors. Audiences and critics were sitting up and taking notice of what was happening in France and Truffaut's career was well and truly underway.

As it turned out, the character of Antoine Doinel would not be confined to just *The 400 Blows.* Truffaut would resurrect him for another four films that followed him through adolescence and into adulthood culminating in *Love on the Run* (*L'Amour en Fuite*) in 1979. In all these films, Antoine was played by Jean-Pierre Léaud in what must be a unique relationship between actor, character and director. The films, which were much lighter in tone than *The 400 Blows,* are among Truffaut's most charming and popular. Antoine Doinel continued to be an alter ego of Truffaut's, sometimes mirroring the director's experiences, but as he grew older Léaud's personality also made its mark. Insiders claim that as the series of films progressed, Antoine Doinel became less like Truffaut and more like Léaud. Because of his work with Truffaut and other directors like Jean-Luc Godard, Léaud became something of a new wave icon. He was certainly one of my favorite French actors of the Sixties.

Truffaut had a busy and largely successful career right up to his early death at 52 in 1984. His films covered a range of subjects but each had his distinctive style. He made a single English language picture – *Fahrenheit 451* in 1966 and presented us with one of the best movies about making movies with *Day for Night* (*La Nuit Américaine*) in 1973 in which he also played the part of a very harassed film director. He enjoyed doing an occasional bit of acting even if it was just a Hitchcock-type cameo and somehow ended up with a part in Steven Spielberg's *Close Encounters of the Third Kind.* Truffaut was a special talent and is greatly missed.

Just as some people do not like black and white movies, there are many who avoid foreign films, especially if they contain subtitles. This is unfortunate because there are many gems in foreign films to be enjoyed. When I was a kid, we thought that French films were all about sex and Brigitte Bardot. I am glad I found out otherwise.

==============================

I'M ALL RIGHT JACK – 1959

A classic British comedy from the prolific Boulting Brothers, *I'm All Right Jack* finds a lot of fun and humor in factory workplaces, left wing unions, and the great British disease, strikes – not to mention the shenanigans of the owners and managers. To American viewers, it seemed like a strange setting for a comedy but the British knew that it was a situation ripe for satire.

The story concerns an Oxford-educated twit who, after failing to find any suitable employment, is persuaded by his conniving uncle to take a lowly job in one of his factories. Of course, the not-too-bright chap is merely a pawn in one of his uncle's unscrupulous deals but he finds he likes the position and even becomes a lodger in the home of the communist-sympathizing shop steward with a sexy daughter. All goes well until the young fellow unknowingly assists a time and motion man by showing off how efficient he can be. New work standards are imposed, a strike is called, and the poor chap is regarded as a traitor by his newfound mates. Of course, this is precisely what his uncle had hoped would happen but then things do not exactly go according to plan. All of this happens with a flurry of typical British humor delivered by a first-rate cast.

Ian Carmichael, who made a career out of playing slightly upper class twits, was the poor unfortunate caught in the middle of everything. His uncle was slyly portrayed by the oily Dennis Price with equally odious Richard Attenborough as his partner in dirty dealings. The role of the factory's manager was entrusted to the always reliable Terry-Thomas and the nervous time and motion man was played by the most familiar face in British movies, John Le Mesurier.

When I was young, John Le Mesurier appeared in so many films – virtually every British movie I saw – that I thought there was some sort of law that required his presence in them.

On the distaff side, there was the great Margaret Rutherford as Carmichael's rich and imposing aunt and the equally great but in a much different way Irene Handl as the harried wife of the chief shop steward. There was a scene between Rutherford and Handl – two strong women from opposite sides of the class system – that was pure magic to behold. Liz Fraser, a popular British sex kitten in those days, more than filled the part as the object of Carmichael's lust.

Dominating these seasoned comedy players was the performance of Peter Sellers as Fred Kite, the lefty shop steward who single-handedly represented everything that was wrong with the trade union movement of the time. His portrait of a man corrupted by a tiny bit of power was priceless and earned him a British Academy

Award as best actor. And Sellers was an actor in those days who relished immersing himself in difficult comedic roles, much like his hero Alec Guinness. Sellers manages the neat trick of making the audience laugh at him and feel sorry for him, on occasion at the same time. It is hard to imagine anyone else delivering a line like "We do not and cannot accept the principle that incompetence justifies dismissal" with a straight face.

Even at this point in his career, Sellers was considered to be very demanding and difficult to work with. He did not always endear himself to his co-stars. Producer Roy Boulting said: "He was his own worst enemy, although there was plenty of competition." Still, he had a great talent and had not yet begun to waste it.

The world was quite different when *I'm All Right Jack* was made and things have changed quite a lot which makes some aspects of the film seem rather dated, in particular the dreadful title song performed with too much enthusiasm by someone named Al Saxon. But human nature and its foibles have not changed and it is in representing them that the film really shines. Margaret Thatcher may have tamed the trade unions but the class system is still alive and well in Britain today. There were some nice little touches in the movie such as beginning and ending it in a nudist colony where Carmichael was the object of the ladies' interest. The film may not have the same bite that it once had but it can still be viewed as a very good comedy and a nostalgic look at a Britain that no longer exists.

I'm All Right Jack was the most popular film in the UK that year which is not surprising considering all the talent that was involved. It is still pretty good today.

==================================

ANATOMY OF A MURDER – 1959

It is hard to believe now that *Anatomy of a Murder* was once considered to be a very daring and shocking movie because it dealt with and even mentioned things such as condoms, rape and panties – and that such a film should star a wholesome figure like James Stewart. In fact, Stewart's father was so disappointed in his son being in what he regarded as a dirty picture that he took out an ad in the local newspaper urging people not to see it. How times have changed.

Anatomy of a Murder was a big, overblown and overlong film by that dictatorial director Otto Preminger whom some said liked to give the appearance of dealing with controversial themes without ever making the mistake of actually doing so. In this film, he created a scandal simply by using a few naughty words.

James Stewart played a supposedly simple small town lawyer who agrees to defend a soldier accused of murdering a popular local man who the soldier claimed had raped his wife. Stewart's usual thoughtful and slow talking performance allowed the audience to sift through the evidence with him as he realized that no one was being totally honest with him, least of all the soldier's rather flirtatious and provocatively attired wife. When the case came to trial – and this is basically a courtroom drama – the prosecution cheats slightly by bringing in a sharp and experienced prosecutor from the big city to help with their case.

While the rest of the cast is made up of familiar faces, they were mostly either actors rather than stars or stars who had not yet made it big. The screenplay by Wendell Mayes provides plenty of juicy roles for the cast to get their teeth into but for the most part the performances are kept relatively low-key to keep things more realistic. A jazzy musical score by Duke Ellington is sometimes catchy but not always appropriate but it was obviously included as another selling point.

Lee Remick was surprisingly sensuous as the defendant's attractive wife while Ben Gazzara was properly harried as her short-tempered and jealous husband. George C. Scott made an early screen appearance as the big city prosecutor in one of his better performances before he turned into a monster. Stewart was ably assisted by sardonic Eve Arden as his loyal secretary and by Arthur O'Connell in an impressive turn as an alcoholic former lawyer whose brain cells have not been completely destroyed by booze. There were also good parts for veteran character actors such as Murray Hamilton and Russ Brown as well as the future Mrs. Bing Crosby, Kathryn Grant. Preminger added a nice touch by having the judge played by an actual judge, Joseph N. Welch. The director was aware of the dangers of casting a non-professional in a key role and supposedly made certain that Welch never had to talk and move at the same time.

The film took its time in getting to the courtroom but when it did everything seemed to get better. It is hard to know what exactly makes courtroom dramas so compelling but they certainly provide actors with an opportunity to shine. It is the only reason I can think of to explain why Gregory Peck won the Oscar for *To Kill A Mockingbird* in the same year that Peter O'Toole was nominated for *Lawrence of Arabia.* As it turned out, Stewart, O'Connell and Scott were all nominated for *Anatomy of a Murder* although none of them won.

Despite its alleged notoriety, the movie was praised for its accurate depiction of trial procedures. The fact that the screenplay was based on a novel by a former Michigan Supreme Court Justice might have helped.

Anatomy of a Murder featured a clever set of opening titles designed by the legendary Saul Bass. Credits of this sort are virtually a lost art – sometimes they were better than the movie that followed them. Personally, I hate the modern practice of superimposing the credits over the first scenes of a film and miss the days when opening titles were creative and helped to set the mood for what was to follow.

The black and white photography helped the audience to concentrate on the dialogue – and there was plenty of dialogue. The Michigan locations were a bonus. One critic said that *Anatomy of a Murder* was a black and white movie that was full of local color.

===================================

SOME LIKE IT HOT – 1959

One of the best movie comedies ever made was Billy Wilder's *Some Like It Hot,* made in glorious black and white. The premise was original: A pair of out of work musicians in Prohibition-era Chicago inadvertently witness a St. Valentine's Day-type of massacre and need to get out of town quick. Their not so obvious solution is to dress up like women and join an all-girl band on its way to a gig at a fancy hotel in Florida where, of course, the mobsters will later be holding a "convention". Along the way, they become friendly with the gorgeous but not very bright singer in the band and, in Florida, one of the cross-dressing musicians attracts the attention of a much older millionaire. In the hands of Wilder and his frequent script collaborator I.A.L. Diamond, the gags and one-liners come thick and fast as the situation of two men permanently trapped in women's clothing is fully exploited.

A number of Hollywood stars turned down the lead roles including Bob Hope, Danny Kaye, Jerry Lewis and even Frank Sinatra. The final choice of Tony Curtis and Jack Lemmon was near perfect as the two stars each took a slightly different approach to being Daphne and Josephine. Lemmon was the more obviously comic while Curtis not only got to imitate Grace Kelly as Daphne but also had an opportunity to slip out of his dress to do a memorable Cary Grant impersonation.

There is a legend that Curtis developed a taste for dressing up and continued to wear women's clothes in private moments. The worst director in history Edward D. Wood Jr., himself a notorious cross-dresser, claimed to have indulged in this fetish with Curtis which partly led to his split with Janet Leigh. There is little evidence to support this but it must be said that Curtis looked very comfortable in drag.

The big attraction in the film was, of course, Marilyn Monroe in one of her best roles as the sexy and naïve dumb blonde destined to always get the fuzzy end of the lollipop. Monroe looked fabulous in *Some Like It Hot* but, by all accounts, was a monster to work with, turning up late and requiring numerous takes for a single line of dialogue. But she was Marilyn. As Billy Wilder said: "I have an old aunt who would be on the set every morning at six and know her lines backwards. But who would go to see her?" Some sources claim that Monroe was pregnant during the filming although she later miscarried. Whatever problems there were, they certainly did not appear on the screen. Monroe was both sexy and delightful.

The ever-gallant Tony Curtis famously said that kissing Monroe was "like kissing Hitler" although he never explained how he knew what kissing Hitler was like.

Apparently, Monroe wanted the movie to be shot in color and even had a standing contract that stated that all of her films should be in color. But black and white suited *Some Like It Hot* because of its 1920s setting and because color tends to slow down comedy. The final decision was made after early tests revealed that Curtis and Lemmon in drag looked grotesque in color.

The gangster-era background was enhanced by the presence of George Raft and Pat O'Brien, two veterans of the old gangster movies. Another old face that made a lasting impression was Joe E. Brown, a former B-movie comic in the best role of his career as the old millionaire lusting after Jack Lemmon. Their "romantic" scenes together are a highlight and Brown gets to deliver the movie's classic final line "Nobody's perfect" which is still regarded as one of the best last lines in film.

There are many great scenes in the film. One of the best is when Monroe and Curtis, dressed as a man and pretending to be a millionaire, are alone on a yacht and Curtis tries the old seduction technique of claiming that women have no effect on him, prompting Monroe to attempt a cure.

Wilder keeps the pace just below frenetic with only an occasional pause to allow Monroe to show off her musical skills and, during her final number, a gown that had to be seen to be believed. *Some Like It Hot* was considered to be something of a naughty film because of Monroe's overt sexiness and the cross-dressing theme but audiences and critics loved it and, perhaps because of its period setting, it does not seem dated at all. At two hours, it is slightly long for a comedy but no one seems to care when they are having so much fun.

==================================

PSYCHO – 1960

The movie that is most usually associated with Alfred Hitchcock is *Psycho* which I consider unfortunate because he made better films such as my favorite Hitchcock movie *North by Northwest.* But *Psycho,* or rather its reputation, looms large in the public imagination as some sort of ultimate scary film. I do not agree with that assessment and admit that I was in two minds about including *Psycho* in this book of classics.

Many people are only familiar with *Psycho* from seeing clips of the justifiably famous shower scene or Martin Balsam climbing the stairs in the old house. There are several very scary sequences in *Psycho.* The problem is that there are a lot of drawn out scenes and too much dialogue to get through in between. Hitchcock used to say that he disliked films that were "pictures of people talking" but he gives us quite a lot of that in *Psycho* and it lets the whole thing down.

Of course, that may have been Hitchcock's intention – bore the hell out of everybody and then give them a sudden shock. Many of the film critics of the time were not impressed. Perhaps they did not appreciate the innovation that *Psycho* was the first American movie to contain a shot of a toilet flushing.

Anthony Perkins, who had a moderately successful career in films such *Friendly Persuasion, Green Mansions* and *On the Beach,* would be forever typecast as a weirdo after playing Norman Bates in *Psycho.* A very shy person off-screen, Perkins managed to introduce an element of creepiness from his very first appearance in the movie. It was not hard to see why the Bates Motel did less than thriving business.

Janet Leigh, an established star, provided the biggest surprise in the film by getting into a shower. She was the reason for Hitchcock's insistence that no one be admitted to the theater after the movie had begun but, of course, everyone now knows what happened to her. The rest of the cast – Vera Miles, Martin Balsam, John Gavin, John McIntire – adequately fulfill their roles without actively engaging the audience. Hitchcock was not known for his rapport with actors. He was however fond of playing somewhat sick practical jokes on them and to treating them to the sight of his navel-less belly.

Psycho was shot fairly quickly on a seemingly low budget because not too many people had faith in the project. The black and white photography kept things properly moody and the atmosphere was greatly helped by a sinister musical score by Bernard Herrmann who used an orchestra comprised only of string instruments to provide a distinctive and eerie sound. Unfortunately, Herrmann could do nothing to relieve the long scenes of dialogue.

In his famous all-encompassing interview with François Truffaut, Hitchcock was asked, in reference to some of his other films, why the characters in trouble did not go to the police. Hitchcock replied that going to the police was boring. In *Psycho,* he proved just how boring that could be with a prolonged visit to see the sheriff which did absolutely nothing to advance the plot.

Something else that always surprised me about *Psycho* was the terrible ending. There is the final shock of discovering Norman's mother and realizing what Norman has been up to. It is a properly climatic moment but instead of ending the movie there the audience is subjected to about five minutes of very dry explanation about everything that has happened. It is a major miscalculation by a film maker who should know better.

Still, if nothing else, there was that tremendous shower scene, one that has been copied and parodied so many times since that it shock value has all but evaporated. The scene has been endlessly dissected until any possible mystery about it has gone. We know all about Janet Leigh's nude body double, that despite various claims a nipple was never seen, that chocolate syrup was used for blood, that opening title designer Saul Bass was somehow involved, that Anthony Perkins was not even there when the scene was shot and that Hitchcock himself may have wielded the knife. There is such a thing as too much information.

Psycho was the first great slasher movie and it spawned several sequels and a very limp remake. It also led to a plethora of gory and excessive imitations for which the demand seems unending. It was not Hitchcock's finest moment but it is apparently his most famous.

===============================

LA DOLCE VITA – 1960

Italian director Federico Fellini explored the postwar decadence of his native country in the extravagant three hour long film *La Dolce Vita* in which, among other things, he introduced the term *paparazzi* to the world. To say that Fellini was self-indulgent is the same as saying a midget is short. He liked to turn his fantasies and his nightmares into movies. So vivid was his imagination that when he tried LSD in the mid-Sixties, he was disappointed that the experience did not match his usual hallucinatory visions. Some critics complained that his films were like cinematic masturbation. Fellini disagreed, saying his movies were acts of real masturbation. His pictures could be fascinating and frustrating to watch in equal measure. I remember once seeing a midnight showing of his *Juliet of the Spirits* and having very strange dreams for several weeks afterwards.

La Dolce Vita was a kind of breakthrough film for Fellini and established his international reputation after the success of his earlier *La Strada*. Some of the credit goes to the lead performance of the magnificent Marcello Mastroianni, one of the great figures of Italian cinema. Despite his usual easy-going manner, Mastroianni was a very intelligent actor who knew how to inhabit his roles. Director Luchoni Visconti noted that "He's never a hero. He's an anti-hero and that is why the public adore him. That's his great merit and appeal." Mastroianni was seldom more appealing than in *La Dolce Vita*.

He worked with a disparate cast that included the statuesque Anita Ekberg, French actress Anouk Aimée, and one-time Tarzan Lex Barker. Apparently, Fellini had tried to get none other than Marilyn Monroe for the Ekberg part but was predictably unsuccessful.

Italian film makers did not worry about having international casts. Until well into the 1970s, it was the usual practice for them to film their movies without sound and to dub in all the dialogue in post-production. Depending on which language was being dubbed, the actors may or may not have dubbed their own voices. It was not uncommon for characters in Italian movies to have voices that did not quite match their appearance. It probably also reduced the need for multiple takes when someone kept flubbing their lines.

Another eccentricity was the Italian habit of filming scenes that should have been exterior in studios. They were quite good at it. Few people ever realized that the famous fountain scene with Ekberg was actually shot in a studio. But then, cinema is all about illusion, isn't it?

From the opening shot of a large statue of Christ being transported by helicopter across Rome to the final seaside scene, the audience knows they are in for something different. Mastroianni's search for love and happiness may or may not have been successful as he spends seven days trawling through the decadent "sweet life" of modern Italian society. Whether that society was actually like that or merely a part of Fellini's imagination we can only guess. The movie has a very loose structure which, with its length, asks a lot from the audience.

Fellini showed us the Italian high life but could never seem to decide if he was for it or against it. Some of his film is satirical while other parts are almost wistful. The world seemed on the cusp of change in 1960 and *La Dolce Vita* was an indication of the way things might possibly go.

Most critics praised *La Dolce Vita* although the film had a few detractors in particular the Catholic Church which roundly condemned it. It was certainly a different kind of movie than American audiences were used to and was primarily exhibited on the arthouse circuit. But the movie's reputation has grown and the film itself is not as dated as it might have been considering it is a record of a bygone era. Video and DVD have made *La Dolce Vita* more accessible even if some of it suffers on the small screen. Many regard it as Fellini's best film – it is certainly not quite as excessive or incomprehensible as some of his later pictures. Both his direction and the screenplay, which he co-wrote, were nominated for Academy Awards but, strangely, the movie itself was not nominated for best foreign language film (Bergman's *Through A Glass Darkly* won) which just shows what a lottery the Oscars are.

===============================

NEVER ON SUNDAY – 1960

Few movies have captured the essence of another country as easily or as enjoyably as *Never on Sunday* did with Greece. A naughty adults-only comedy that was really not all that naughty – certainly not by today's standards - in which the main character was a carefree and popular prostitute who plied her trade in the port of Piraeus. She was a typical whore with a heart of gold who nevertheless had her own set of standards. They were low but she had them.

Filmed with a mixture of Greek and English dialogue, the film followed an ingenuous American tourist – a lover of all things Greek – as he discovers that Greek culture has moved on a bit since the days of Socrates and Euripides. His culture shock comes in the form of the shameless prostitute Illya, a temptress who does not have to try very hard to be tempting.

Melina Mercouri, who played Illya, was not so much beautiful as she was sensuous with a smoky voice and wild, fiery eyes. Her body language seldom left any doubt about what was on her mind. She was quite happy to be naughty and very often she was naughty to be happy. Most of the men in the port knew her in the biblical sense as did many a visiting sailor, but not on Sundays when she held a kind of open house to entertain her many friends in other ways.

Running headlong into this salacious whirlwind was Homer, just off the boat from America and full of ideas about Greece that he had only acquired from books. He is fascinated by Illya but does not want to be just another one of her customers. Instead, with the misplaced enthusiasm of an alleged intellectual, he decides to educate Illya and to show her the error of her ways. This does not make Homer a very popular person in Piraeus.

Homer is played by the movie's writer and director Jules Dassin. He and Mercouri had been a couple since the mid-Fifties, eventually married in the mid-Sixties, and were together until her death in 1994. They had made a few films together prior to *Never on Sunday* but not with the same amount of success. Dassin had been a notable Hollywood director of movies such as *The Canterville Ghost* and *The Naked City* until he ran afoul of the McCarthy witch-hunts. He then moved to France where he directed the classic heist movie *Rififi.* His work on *Never on Sunday* was among his best and his performance as the earnest moral crusader was a perfect foil for Mercouri's nonchalant immorality.

In many ways, the film prefers to be comic rather than philosophical which adds to its delight. Many of the characters are broadly drawn but this suits the purpose of the production. The supporting cast are all Greek – very Greek – and the location shooting beautifully captures the Greek atmosphere. When I first saw *Never on Sunday,* I thought the Greek background – the taverna, the music, the people – must be exaggerated. But years later I was able to visit a number of Greek islands on various holidays and I found people and places that were exactly like those in the film, although I never encountered anyone quite like Illya.

The music in *Never on Sunday* by Manos Hatzidakis is just as much an essential ingredient as the two main performances. The catchy title song went on to be a big hit which is still regularly played in Greek holiday resorts everywhere. It also won the Oscar for best song. But in addition to the song was the wonderful bouzouki music that is heard throughout the picture, especially when everyone starts to dance in the taverna.

Melina Mercouri won the best actress award at the Cannes Film Festival for *Never on Sunday.* She and Dassin made some more films together including *Phaedra* in 1962 and *Topkapi* in 1964. Mercouri reprised her most famous role on Broadway in the musical *Illya Darling* in 1967. She eventually turned from films to the stage then became the rather outspoken Greek Minister for Culture in 1981.

Never on Sunday was considered quite risqué in 1960 but seems fairly tame today. That has not lessened the enjoyment it provides. It is difficult not to regard Illya as a heroine despite her profession. She was one of the first really liberated women of the Sixties. And, for me, *Never on Sunday* showed a naïve adolescent boy just how sexy a black bra could be.

==================================

LOLITA – 1962

"However did they make a film of *Lolita*?" asked the movie posters. The answer, most probably, was not very easily. The film's origin was a rather scandalous novel by Vladimir Nabokov and it seemed certain that, in order to reach the screen, the screenplay – also by Nabokov – would have to make some changes. And there were.

The story was far from the usual Hollywood fare. It concerned a stuffy, middle-aged academic's obsession with a very young girl. In the book, the "nymphet" was twelve but the movie increased her age to fourteen on the theory that would somehow make things better. The central character, an English professor named Humbert Humbert, was played – or rather typically underplayed – by James Mason. At the time, many observers thought the role would be perfect for the dissolute Errol Flynn given his well-publicized taste for young females but Flynn, always a contrary person, spoiled that juicy bit of casting by dying – the result of his "wicked, wicked ways."

If the main character was an eccentric, it was only fitting that *Lolita* be directed by another genuine weirdo in the form of Stanley Kubrick. While other directors turned the project down without a second thought, Kubrick embraced it with open arms. Kubrick was a perfectionist with enough quirks for two or three people. He liked to have his own way. One actor who worked with him complained: "Just because you're a perfectionist doesn't mean you're perfect."

Although Kubrick had been widely praised for his direction of *Spartacus* in 1960, he was not happy with the interference he had both from the studio and from producer and star Kirk Douglas. He left Hollywood never to return and set up shop in England, a country with a known tolerance for eccentrics. That, coupled with his fear of flying, led to him making all his subsequent films in Britain, no matter where they were set. Although set in America, most of *Lolita* was shot in England and occasionally looks it.

The apparently coveted role of Lolita was given to fourteen year old Sue Lyon whose figure had already blossomed into womanhood and whose pretty face was capable of incredible blankness. Lolita's mother, who had designs on Humbert herself, was played by Shelley Winters in the sort of loud, brassy role that would become her trademark. Lurking on the fringes of the action was a mysterious character called Clare Quilty who was played by Peter Sellers in a performance that allowed him to employ several different voices and disguises.

Pedophilia was not the hot topic in 1962 that it is today but *Lolita* still managed to make some people feel rather uncomfortable. It is perhaps fortunate that there was still some form of censorship in place in those days.

In fact, there was a remake of *Lolita* in 1997, directed by Adrian Lynne and starring Jeremy Irons which failed to find a distributor, reportedly because of the film's subject matter but also possibly because it was a really bad movie. It finally had its premiere on cable television before making its way onto video where it could be enjoyed, or at least watched, in the privacy of one's home.

It is difficult to imagine anyone wanting to marry Shelley Winters just so they could be close to Sue Lyon but that is what James Mason did in *Lolita* – at least until Peter Sellers threw a spanner in the works. Kubrick takes his time in unfolding this not very romantic saga – the film runs about two and a half hours – and works hard to hold the interest of the audience and leaving a fair bit to their imagination. He played fast and loose with Nabokov's screenplay, making substantial changes that did not always follow the original book. Strangely enough, Nabokov did not seem to mind. He was probably happy that sales of the book would increase because of the film. As it turned out, the screenplay was the one thing in the movie that got an Oscar nomination.

Lolita, primarily because of its notorious reputation, was a fair success with audiences but the critical response was divided among those who liked it, those who were offended by it, and those who chose to ignore it altogether. As often happens, the movie has been re-evaluated as the years went by and in more enlightened or at least more permissive times has come to be regarded as one of Kubrick's better efforts. It certainly has not hurt the sale of heart-shaped sunglasses. Kubrick had yet to make his most famous films but with *Lolita* he was well and truly on his way.

===============================

HUD – 1963

Paul Newman made a number of black and white movies in the late Fifties and early Sixties through which he finally managed to shake off comparisons with Marlon Brando as well as obliterating memories of his embarrassing screen debut in the 1954 minor epic *The Silver Chalice*. Choosing just one of those films for this collection was difficult with 1961's *The Hustler* being the front runner. But then I decided on *Hud* because I felt it was more representative of Newman's work in the days when he relished being an anti-hero.

Hud was based on a novel by Larry McMurtry and set in the heart of Texas cattle country where the title character helped to run a ranch, when he was not out getting drunk and chasing women, with his no-nonsense father and impressionable young nephew. Hud was not a likeable character – it was established very early on that he was a selfish bastard – but Newman gives a performance that digs beneath the surface.

Newman has very strong support from veteran Melvyn Douglas as his father and Patricia Neal as their world-weary housekeeper. Both of them won Oscars for their performances. The fourth member of the lead quartet was Brandon de Wilde as the young nephew who hero-worships Newman until he sees him in action once too often.

The film was directed in a straightforward, non-Sixties style by Martin Ritt who let the characters and their environment speak for themselves. The content of *Hud* upset a lot of people, not just for the lack of morals of the title character but also for the use of some language that was still rare in a movie in those days and an attempted rape scene that was just a tad too realistic for comfort.

The atmospheric cinematography was by James Wong Howe who specialized in black and white films and won an Oscar for *Hud* which he considered his best work. There was a very sparse but effective musical score by Elmer Bernstein that was in keeping with the low-key mood of the picture.

Newman prowls and scowls his way through the film, being vaguely charming one moment and thoroughly menacing the next. When the cattle on the ranch are found to be infected with foot and mouth disease, he argues with his father who wants to do the right thing as opposed to looking for a less than honest way out. The confrontation leads to Newman plotting to take over from his aging father. In Hud's opinion, the world and the western way of life have changed, and not for the better, and he fully intends to keep up with the times. "There's so much crap in this world," he says at one point, "You're going to wallow in it sooner or later, like it or not."

Newman later said that he played the role like a villain and was amazed to discover that some members of the younger generation regarded the character as a hero.

The film was very well received by the critics who praised the performances in particular. They may not have been too thrilled with the storyline but they loved the actors. Audiences felt much the same way but then the Sixties were very much the time of the anti-hero and it would be difficult to find a character who was more anti than Paul Newman in *Hud.* Needless to say, the movie has far less shock value today than in 1963 but it is still capable of packing a considerable punch.

It says a lot for Newman's talent that he was able to progress from the thoroughly unpleasant Hud to the affable Butch Cassidy in just six years. But then Newman always had a fairly wide range and turned up in all sorts of movies including comedies and a Hitchcock thriller. He also became famous for his salad dressing and once ruefully remarked: "The embarrassing thing is that the salad dressing is out-grossing my films."

Hud has been called a revisionist western but it is really not so much a western as a Texas-based character study with some very good dialogue by script writers Irving Ravetch and Harriet Frank – the sort of dialogue that actors love. It is not a picture than can be enjoyed exactly but it can be watched with great interest and admiration for the skill of everyone involved. *Hud* was very much a film of its time. I remember seeing it for the first time when it was released and thinking about it for days afterwards. It has been years since I last watched it – it is probably time to see it again.

===================================

DR. STRANGELOVE – 1963

Dr. Strangelove: Or How I Learned to Stop Worrying and Love the Bomb – to give the movie its full title – was a one of a kind film that could probably only have been made in the Sixties when the Cold War was at its height and movies were just beginning to exercise their newfound freedoms. A film about a crazed American general ordering his B-52 bombers to attack Russia – an act that will result in nuclear war and the destruction of the planet – might not seem like the basis for a comedy but that is what *Dr. Strangelove* is, a very dark comedy indeed.

Director Stanley Kubrick later said: "I started work on the screenplay with every intention of making the film a serious treatment. Ideas kept coming to me which I would discard because they were so ludicrous. I kept saying to myself: 'I can't do this. People will laugh.' But after a month or so I began to realize that all the things I was throwing out were the things which were most truthful."

The movie was based on a novel called *Red Alert* by Peter George who got a credit on the screenplay along with Kubrick and Terry Southern. The script treads a fine line between possible reality and obvious insanity. It must be remembered that in 1963 nuclear destruction was a very real possibility – the Cuban missile crisis was still very fresh in everyone's memory. A comedy about the Cold War suddenly becoming very hot was a little bit outrageous to say the least. But people did laugh at it, even if it was occasionally a rather nervous laughter.

In the same year, a movie called *Fail-Safe* was released which treated a very similar scenario seriously. It is interesting that audiences preferred the black humor version to the straight one.

One of the strong points of *Dr. Strangelove* is that the cast more or less played it straight. Sterling Hayden as General Jack Ripper who started the whole thing is a very calm and focused psychopath obsessed with stopping the Communist conspiracy to corrupt his precious bodily fluids. George C. Scott, by contrast, goes way over the top as the president's senior military advisor, another ardent anti-Communist, who manages to be both funny and scary at the same time. Old cowboy star Slim Pickens is an inspired choice to be the pilot of a B-52 with a single-minded determination to carry out his orders. Keenan Wynn has a nice cameo as a combat officer paranoid about "preverts" and Peter Bull is effective as the Russian ambassador. There is even an early role for James Earl Jones as one of the bomber crew and Tracy Reed, stepdaughter of director Carol Reed, gets to look very fetching in a bikini.

But, of course, the movie is dominated by Peter Sellers who plays three roles – the President, an RAF group captain, and the title character. According to some sources, he was also set to play the bomber pilot but, luckily for Slim Pickens and us, was content with just three parts. In many ways, *Dr. Strangelove* was the apex of Sellers' career, coming just before *The Pink Panther* and true international stardom. As the President and the group captain, Sellers gave a remarkable performance as a comic actor – his phone call to the Russian premier was one of the finest scenes he ever did – and it was only as Dr. Strangelove that he went brilliantly to the edge of excess.

Sellers received an Oscar nomination as best actor for his efforts as did the film, screenplay and direction but it failed to win any of them.

As usual, Kubrick made the movie in England and shot it in different aspect ratios, giving some scenes an almost newsreel appearance. The surreal feeling of the film was certainly helped by the stark and occasionally dark black and white photography and the choice of background music – particularly Vera Lynn singing "We'll Meet Again" at the finale – was nicely effective.

I was in high school when *Dr. Strangelove* came out and all my friends thought it was brilliant but it met with somewhat mixed reactions from the older generation. It is mainly viewed now as a very funny black comedy by people who never had the experience of living through the Cold War. That particular edge is now lost but the film still remains a triumph of off the wall cinema. An odd aspect has been added in that now some viewers see Sellers' performance as the President as being very similar to the first President Bush.

Dr. Strangelove is my favorite Kubrick film. As far as I am concerned, he went downhill after that.

==============================

A HARD DAY'S NIGHT – 1964

It was the British who paved the way for the very distinctive Swinging Sixties style of film making with movies such as the Oscar-winning *Tom Jones* in 1963 and the Beatles' first foray into motion pictures the following year. Rock 'n' roll movies were usually low budget affairs because no one thought the phenomenon or the artists involved would last very long. Executives in the music and film industries believed the Beatles were simply a passing fad. To quickly cash in on their popularity, *A Hard Day's Night* was shot in just six weeks on a modest budget. It was said that the bosses at United Artists were more interested in the movie's soundtrack album than the picture itself. They had not reckoned on the aspirations of the young American director working in Britain who was assigned the project, Richard Lester. Far from making the usual rock 'n' roll picture, Lester went for an anarchic comedy that took advantage of the Fab Four's lack of acting talent while showcasing their very popular music.

Lester's background was mostly in television so he was accustomed to a tight shooting schedule. He was a big fan of handheld cameras and often wielded one himself to get the shot he wanted. He loved odd angles and preferred to shot in very short takes that could then be edited together in a fast-paced and almost frenetic manner. His style seemed to suit the Beatles and took everybody by surprise with its seeming freshness and bang up to date modernity which many interpreted as being innovative or avant-garde. It was certainly not what the legions of adolescent girls who made up the majority of the Beatles' fans were expecting. All they really wanted was to see their heroes on the big screen.

I remember it was useless trying to see *A Hard Day's Night* in a movie theater when it first came out because of all the screaming girls in the audience. Most of them only knew the Beatles from their records or seeing them on the Ed Sullivan show. It was a revelation for them to hear the Beatles speak and for most it was their first encounter with a Liverpool accent. Consequently, every time a Beatle opened his mouth, the girls screamed and the dialogue, some of which was quite funny, was totally drowned out.

The script by Alun Owen was a loosely-structured "day in the life" saga in which the Beatles played themselves. The Beatles delivered their bits of dialogue so casually that many thought they were ad-libbing. To offset their amateurish performances, Lester surrounded them with real actors that could hold scenes together and interact with the apparently bemused stars. These included Wilfrid Brambell, best known for the television sitcom *Steptoe and Son,* as Paul McCartney's disreputable grandfather ("He's very clean, isn't he?") who seemed to understand exactly what Lester was looking for, short

Norman Rossington and tall John Junkin as the Beatles' harassed manager and his dim assistant, and Victor Spinetti as a television director on the verge of a nervous breakdown. Just for good measure, there were also cameos by established actors such as Anna Quayle, Kenneth Haigh and Richard Vernon although they went over the heads of most of the audience.

The Beatles themselves were surprisingly good, probably because they did not take the enterprise too seriously. For the first time, their fans were able to see their distinctive personalities or even, in some cases, finally figure out which was which. One contemporary critic rather pretentiously declared that George Harrison had the makings of a first-class screen comic but it was Ringo Starr who got a solo acting spot when he went on a wander by himself. John Lennon, meanwhile, was content to display his slightly surreal sense of humor.

In the old days, comedies like those of the Marx Brothers ground to a halt for musical numbers but in *A Hard Day's Night* the songs were the highlights and the reason for making the film in the first place. The success of the movie exceeded all expectations and a second Beatles film, this time in color, was planned immediately, again with Richard Lester at the helm. Both movies have held up reasonably well as newer generations have discovered them and at least now everyone can hear the dialogue as well as the songs.

John Lennon and Ringo Starr both had short-lived acting careers but *A Hard Day's Night* launched Richard Lester onto the international scene with a series of movies in his characteristic style which, for better or worse, finally lost favor in the Seventies.

==================================

THE AMERICANIZATION OF EMILY – 1964

Some readers may have noticed an absence of war films in this collection. Instead, I have included one of the best anti-war movies ever made: *The Americanization of Emily.* Made at a time when memories of World War Two were still fresh in many minds and when the conflict in Vietnam was in the early stages of escalation, this extremely cynical movie attacked the sacred cows of patriotism and heroism in a biting yet largely humorous way that was difficult to argue with.

Based on a novel by William Bradford Huie, the screenplay was the work of Paddy Chayefsky, a writer noted for a successful career in television drama where his sharp wit and liberal views stood out from the usual fare. The film is basically a love story in which British and American cultural differences are quite obvious but pale into insignificance against the background of World War Two and, specifically, the D-Day landings.

In one of the best roles of his career – and apparently a personal favorite of his – James Garner played the aide to a crotchety old admiral stationed in London in the days leading up to the invasion of Europe. He was what was known as a "dog robber" – an officer capable of procuring virtually anything and ensuring that his boss (and himself) led quite a comfortable life. He is casually amoral and good at his job with not a twinge of conscience until he meets the English girl assigned to be his driver. She is very moral and a bit of a prig but, as often happens in the movies, opposites attract.

Their cozy affair is interrupted when the old admiral has a mental meltdown and decides that the first dead man on Omaha Beach should be a sailor and that Garner should be there to film it. Garner is understandably horrified at the prospect of going on a suicide mission as a publicity stunt for the Navy.

Garner, fresh from his success on television in *Maverick* has seldom been better in a movie and is quite believable in his attempts to make cowardice a virtue. Veteran Hollywood star Melvyn Douglas is impressive as the admiral going from reasonably sane to bonkers and back again. James Coburn shines in an early role as another officer who is converted from the easy life to being a gung-ho militant.

The great surprise of the film is Julie Andrews as Emily. She was between her stage successes in *My Fair Lady* and *Camelot* and her sugary sweet movie roles in *Mary Poppins* and *The Sound of Music.* Viewers who only know her from those kind of pictures will be amazed at how good she is in *The Americanization of Emily,* giving a quite excellent performance as the romantic war widow. She is even, dare I say it, somewhat sexy at times. It is a pity she did not make more movies like this.

As a bonus, there is the delightfully eccentric Joyce Grenfell as Emily's dotty mother and British sex kitten Liz Fraser as another driver in the motor pool. Reliable character actor Keenan Wynn also makes an appearance.

My father was in the US Navy in World War Two and loved *The Americanization of Emily* because he said it accurately portrayed what the Navy brass was really like. Not surprisingly, the film makers received zero cooperation from the Navy.

Paddy Chayefsky's script was the sort that gives the audience something to think about in between the laughs and the clinches between Garner and Andrews. Arthur Hiller directs the picture with a sure hand and is happy to step back and let the characters and dialogue do most of the work. The one anomaly that always struck me was the presence of Garner and Coburn in such a blatantly anti-war piece when just the year before they had both been in *The Great Escape,* a movie that seems to view warfare in quite a different way. I suppose that is what actors call versatility.

The film was very well received by the critics with the performances of Garner and Andrews and the irreverent screenplay attracting much of the praise. Despite the movie's many virtues, it seems to have disappeared somewhat over the years which is unfortunate because it remains an insightful portrait of people and motives. Whether it is a comedy with dramatic overtones or a drama with comic and romantic interludes, it is a film worth seeing – and listening to – if only for the radiant presence of James Garner and Julie Andrews.

===============================

THE NIGHT OF THE IGUANA – 1964

Tennessee Williams is one of my favorite playwrights but, largely because of censorship, he has not always been well served by the movies. That is not to say that films such as *A Streetcar Named Desire* (1951) and *Cat on a Hot Tin Roof* (1958) were not good, only that they were watered down versions of the originals. *The Night of the Iguana* was also toned down a bit and lost a subplot involving Germans but it remains, in my opinion anyway, the most successful transition of Tennessee Williams from stage to screen. A lot of the credit for this belongs to director and writer John Huston.

Huston managed to make the play cinematic, partly through his script and direction and partly as a result of his decision to make the film on location in Mexico. Despite the exotic and colorful locale, he opted to shoot in black and white which would be less distracting and allow the audience to concentrate on the characters and dialogue that were the heart and soul of the production.

Today, the town of Puerto Vallarta is a busy and popular tourist resort but in 1964 it was a sleepy little village that was not easily accessible. It was not a comfortable shoot for cast and crew but the gregarious Huston managed to keep everyone's spirits up and got the results he wanted. *The Night of the Iguana* was one of Huston's better films and even Tennessee Williams, who was a frequent visitor to the set, seemed pleased with the finished film.

In such a project, casting is everything. As the disgraced man of the cloth T. Lawrence Shannon, Richard Burton seemed a logical choice but, in fact, the role had first been offered to actors such as Marlon Brando, James Garner, Burt Lancaster and William Holden. As it turned out, Huston was lucky to have Burton who gave one of his best screen performances. Burton still wanted to be an actor in those days before fame and the need to make money overtook him. He was still largely associated with his notorious affair with Elizabeth Taylor – and she was a constant presence on location – but he managed to curb his more excessive theatrical tendencies and delivered a multi-layered, insightful and even moving performance.

Matching him were two quite different females. One was the quietly demure Deborah Kerr as a panhandling artist who travelled the world with her ninety-eight year old poet grandfather. Kerr's careful unplaying provided the perfect foil to Burton's flamboyance. Playing somewhere in between was Ava Gardner who finally had a chance to act instead of being mere set decoration. Her recently widowed hotel owner, who soothed her grief with a pair of smiling cabana boys, was earthy and sensuous and complemented the performances of the other two stars with her wild looks and sharp tongue.

These three performances make *The Night of the Iguana* as they draw the audience deep into their inner souls. Also involved was Sue Lyon, slightly more grown up since *Lolita,* as a teenaged temptress who would have driven the defrocked minister to drink if he were not already an alcoholic. Small and seemingly frail Cyril Delevanti played Kerr's grandfather with a touching wistfulness. There was also impressive support from Grayson Hall as an extremely repressed lesbian who is Burton's nemesis and who also has designs on Lyon although she will not admit it to herself. Hall's strong performance in such distinguished company was good enough to earn her an Academy Award nomination.

Huston carefully builds the tension that leads to the climatic night of the title during which Burton spends a fair amount of time tied to a hammock, demonstrating that he really only needed his voice and his eyes to deliver a great performance. The actors seemed to love speaking Williams' trademark dialogue which has a strange sort of poetic touch to it. It can also be sharply cynical. At one point, good girl Kerr chides Burton: "There are worse things than chastity" to which he immediately shoots back: "Yes, lunacy and death."

The film was generally well received and did good business, perhaps partly due to some notoriety surrounding it and gossip about what went on during the location shooting. But many people appreciated *The Night of the Iguana* for its intelligence and emotion – it was difficult not to become involved with its characters. I consider the movie to be an old friend and watch with pleasure at least once a year.

================================

DARLING – 1965

In many ways, *Darling* is the quintessential Sixties flick. It certainly established Julie Christie as an icon of that decade. With its flashy photography, jump cut editing, stylish costumes, cynical dialogue, a jazz and pop background score, locations in swinging London, Paris and Italy, and occasionally an almost *cinéma vérité* style, *Darling* was the epitome of what was happening – or perceived to be happening – in that wild and crazy era. Detractors say that the film has dated badly but it was never meant to be more than a reflection of its time.

The title character is an amoral and self-centered model who prefers sex to talent as a means of furthering her career. She is not, it must be said, a very likeable person (nor are most of the characters in *Darling*) but Christie manages to inject enough humanity in her to make the audience care about her or, at least, to stick around long enough to find out what happens next.

The screenplay was by Frederic Raphael, a sharp-tongued writer whose characters are invariably witty and never lost for a clever retort. His view of the swinging set was that of either a very new member or someone on the outside looking in. In either case, he was not impressed by what he had seen and his portrait of London in the Sixties, while fascinating, was not particularly flattering.

Directing everything in a style that would soon become synonymous with the decade was John Schlesinger in what was only his third feature film. With a modest budget and a lot of imagination, he put together a movie that, at least in parts, had a tendency to stick in one's memory.

Schlesinger was fortunate in his three stars who, in addition to Christie, included Dirk Bogarde and Laurence Harvey. Christie had made an impressive and all too brief appearance in Schlesinger's *Billy Liar* in 1963. Now she was the whole movie and deservedly so. Bogarde masterfully underplayed his part as the intellectual who makes the mistake of falling in love with Christie and is probably the only character to evoke some sympathy. It is usual practice to knock Laurence Harvey but he could be very effective in the right part and with the right script and *Darling* provided both.

Various sources claim that Shirley MacLaine was set to play the lead but backed out while the Bogarde part had first been offered to none other Gregory Peck. We can be thankful that the main cast remained an all-British affair even if they were not such big box office draws in America. As it turned out, *Darling* did very good business in the States and both Christie and Raphael picked up Oscars for their work, as did Julie Harris for her costume designs.

Although I first saw *Darling* in Baltimore in the Sixties, it was not until I moved to the UK some twenty years later that I saw the uncensored version. For the American market, a sequence at a Parisian orgy was noticeably trimmed and when Christie later had a nude scene, the screen was suddenly cropped and a bit grainy. After a while, I realized that the foreign films I saw in my younger days were not necessarily intact.

In some ways, *Darling* and the character of Diana Scott anticipate the ridiculous cult of celebrity that was to come. At one point, Christie's character even becomes Princess Diana. Similarly, the Laurence Harvey character and his milieu hint at the coming of figures like Tony Blair and a very different Britain. Was Raphael being prophetic or merely cynical?

In recent years, John Schlesinger has tended to distance himself from his earlier movies and from *Darling* in particular. I always find it unfortunate and a bit sad when film makers do this, as if they are embarrassed by the past. Of course, people and tastes change but there is little point in regretting past mistakes, especially if they are not considered mistakes by everyone.

Christie, Schlesinger and Raphael made another picture together – the poorly received *Far From the Madding Crowd* – before Schlesinger crossed the Atlantic to win an Oscar for directing *Midnight Cowboy.* Julie Christie found even bigger fame in *Doctor Zhivago* and continued making films, some of which were strange choices.

A lot of years have passed and I can only wonder what people who were not alive in the Sixties think when they view *Darling.* Hopefully, they will accept it for what it is – a brilliant portrait of a time that passed too quickly.

===========================

REPULSION – 1965

One of the scariest movies ever made was this psychological shocker by Roman Polanski, his first English language film. Polanski had arrived on the scene in 1962 with the Polish film *Knife in the Water* after which he left his native country and set up camp in Paris. There he and Gérard Brach developed the story and screenplay for *Repulsion* in the hope the movie would be sufficiently successful to fund their more ambitious project *Cul de Sac*. As it turned out, *Repulsion* was the better film with the better reputation. It is still regarded as one of Polanski's best movies.

It is unclear why Polanski decided to make the movie in London and in English. It was probably with an eye to a wider audience as well as having more opportunities to secure finance. As it turned out, the film was backed by a company that mostly made softcore porn pictures, not that that would have bothered Polanski.

The beautiful French actress Catherine Deneuve plays a young Belgian girl who lives in a London flat with her older sister and her sister's boyfriend. She has an unfulfilling job as a manicurist and does not make friends easily. When her sister goes away on holiday, Deneuve is left all alone and that is when the trouble begins. Mentally fragile to begin with, the solitude and her own feelings, particularly towards men, lead to a gradual psychological decline as she tries to cope with loneliness, nightmares and an extremely claustrophobic environment. A would-be suitor forces his way into the flat to declare his love for her and is bludgeoned to death with a candlestick. Later, the lecherous landlord tries to force himself on her and meets a similar fate. The girl is clearly not interested in having sex with anyone.

Polanski is not concerned so much with why Deneuve is having a breakdown or is so repulsed by men, although there is a vague suggestion of paternal abuse, as to how it happens. He heightens the threatening atmosphere with tight camerawork and exaggerated sound effects of things like clocks and hearts as well as creating hallucinations and dream sequences to unnerve both Deneuve and the viewer. Perhaps the most memorable of these is when Deneuve tries to make her way down a narrow hallway when suddenly a number of hands and arms emerge out of the walls to grab and grope her.

My darling and impressionable wife made the mistake of first seeing *Repulsion* on a late night television showing when she was alone in her little London flat. To say that it scared the hell out of her would be an understatement yet, for some reason, she watched it until the end. She found the hallway scene especially frightening. To this day, I can always get a scream out of her in any narrow passageway. She refuses to see *Repulsion* again and does not even like to talk about it. I suspect Polanski would consider that to be a measure of his success.

In some ways, *Repulsion* is the flip side of "swinging" London from films like *Darling.* The location shooting make for a realistic background and also provide a more than capable supporting cast including Ian Hendry, John Fraser, Yvonne Furneaux and Patrick Wymark. Polanski was also proud that *Repulsion* contained the first audio of a female orgasm in a British movie.

To help get Deneuve in the proper skittish and unnerved mood, Polanski insisted that she remain celibate for the duration of the filming. He personally arranged for her accommodation and ensured that she was never left alone with a member of the opposite sex. Deneuve's feelings about all this are not known but she gave a powerful performance in the film, proving that it is possible for someone to be a beautiful movie star and a convincing actress at the same time.

Roman Polanski is a strange little chap with a vivid imagination and an overactive libido. He has had a colorful and occasionally tragic private life that was not always so private. Since the late 1970s, because of legal hassles, he has lived and worked in Europe. He is responsible for an impressive array of movies such as *Rosemary's Baby, Chinatown* and *The Pianist* as well as the off the wall comedy *The Fearless Vampire Killers* in which he also starred with his doomed wife Sharon Tate.

Repulsion is a creepy and frightening movie. Unlike most of today's thrillers, it is more psychological than gory and should never be watched alone.

==================================

THE LOVED ONE – 1965

The movie with something to offend everyone was British director Tony Richardson's follow-up to his very successful, Oscar-winning film *Tom Jones* in 1963. Based on a book by Evelyn Waugh as well as Jessica Mitford's *The American Way of Death*, the screenplay by notorious *Candy* author Terry Southern and British novelist Christopher Isherwood delighted in taking potshots at the excesses in American culture and in particular the California funeral business. The mixture of dark humor and satire was never going to please everybody and the film quickly became one of those love it or hate it affairs.

To play the young English protagonist, Richardson cast American actor Robert Morse who was best known for having starred in the hit Broadway musical *How to Succeed in Business Without Really Trying,* itself a satire on modern America. Although Morse was uncomfortable with both his accent and his Beatles-style haircut (still rare in America at that time) he gave a superb comic performance that held together the various threads of the movie's plot. He, in fact, had so much trouble maintaining an English accent that all his dialogue had to be re-recorded and dubbed in post-production. While he may have seemed an odd choice for the role as a Brit dazed and confused in Hollywood, he made it work.

Morse was in some illustrious if eclectic company. The best among them is John Gielgud as a stately but disillusioned artist ground down by the Hollywood studio system to the point that he hangs himself, thus necessitating the need to shift the scene to the opulent Whispering Glades cemetery. There he is worked on by head undertaker Rod Steiger, a marginally unhinged man with an unusual home life and a lustful eye on a beautician who provides make-up for dead people and loves her job. Playing two roles is the wonderful Jonathan Winters as the megalomaniac owner of Whispering Glades with big plans for the future ("There has got to be a way to get those stiffs off my property") and his less successful brother who runs a funeral service for pets and gives Morse a job.

Gielgud is sublime and Winters is a hoot in both roles but Steiger, as usual, tends to overact and almost throws things off-balance. Along the way there are cameo parts for familiar faces such as James Coburn, Roddy McDowell, Robert Morley, Milton Berle, Tab Hunter, Lionel Stander and Liberace as an enthusiastic coffin salesman, a role he seemed born to play. Diminutive twenty-five year old Paul Williams plays an adolescent who is also a genius with rockets. Putting bodies into orbit becomes a real possibility.

The female lead was unknown Anjanette Comer, a pretty girl with a sense of the ridiculous. Living in a condemned house overhanging a cliff, she is torn between the affections of Morse, who she thinks is a poet, and Steiger, who she works with and respects. Her solution to her dilemma, in part prompted by advice from a newspaper agony aunt who is really an unfeeling man, provides a very strange climatic moment, the details of which we will not go into here.

Even for the Sixties, *The Loved One* was a weird picture and, not surprisingly, received a very mixed reaction. Richardson was reportedly delighted when studio executives walked out of a screening in disgust but, unfortunately, a lot of critics felt the same way which did not help ticket sales. Some of us who were young and rebellious in 1965, loved the movie because it was so outrageous. It was probably somewhat ahead of its time. While a movie like *Dr. Strangelove* could make us laugh at our own fears, *The Loved One* made a comedy of extreme bad taste out of the ultimate dread – death.

I will admit I could have done without the scenes involving Steiger's grossly obese mother but the orgy in the coffin showroom was an image that even Ken Russell probably never would have conceived. Jonathan Winters in the role of the Blessed Reverend attempting to seduce Comer with the aid of his "living statues" while declaring "Beauty in every form!" is a vision that is not easily forgotten. In fact, once seen *The Loved One* lingers in the memory which is either the sign of a good movie or a very bad dream.

The Loved One is pretty much a cult film. It was not entirely successful but it hit more targets than it missed. It is easy to dismiss it as just another weird and wonderful Sixties flick but it was slightly more than that although no one is quite sure what.

==============================

THE LAST PICTURE SHOW – 1971

By the 1970s, black and white movies were becoming a rarity but a few film makers occasionally insisted that black and white was the best look for their pictures. Film critic turned director Peter Bogdanovich ignored a multitude of objections to making *The Last Picture Show* in the subdued shades of black and white that he wanted. In the end, he was proven right.

The movie was based on a novel by Larry McMurtry with the screenplay a collaboration between Bogdanovich and McMurtry. It was set in a small Texas town in the early 1950s and contained a twinge of nostalgia that lamented the passing of a way of life. While some of it is a coming of age story concerning recent high school graduates, the film also makes time for the older generation and their relationships and problems. The story is occasionally bleak, even tragic, but it is wonderfully observed and beautifully acted.

The focal point of the film is a trio of attractive youngsters played by Timothy Bottoms, Jeff Bridges, and Cybill Shepherd in her first film. Bottoms, despite his unfortunate surname, was a somewhat under-rated actor who was capable of very sensitive performances and he gives one here. Bridges at this early stage of his career demonstrates the talent that he will develop as that career progresses. Former model Shepherd looks lovely and even does a rather daring nude scene but her acting range was limited. That did not stop Bogdanovich falling in love with her and starring her in several more movies during their relationship.

The real acting honors, however, went to some of the older members of the cast. Among them was veteran cowboy Ben Johnson who played the worldly wise owner of the local pool hall, movie theater, and café and who acts as a sort of mentor to the boys. Cloris Leachman, who was best known for her comedy role in television's *Mary Tyler Moore Show,* surprised everyone with her poignant portrayal of the neglected wife of the high school football coach who has an affair with Bottoms. Other performers in this ensemble piece were Eileen Brennan as an earthy waitress, Ellen Burstyn as Shepherd's mother, Clu Gulager as Burstyn's lover who also ends up in bed with Shepherd, and an early role for Randy Quaid as a well-to-do nerd.

When Oscar time rolled around, *The Last Picture Show* missed out on best picture and best director but scooped up the best supporting actor gong for Ben Johnson and the best supporting actress award for Cloris Leachman, both of which were richly deserved.

The movie took advantage of the permissive mood in the movies during the Seventies and used language and situations that would not have been allowed even ten years earlier. There is a lot of sex in *The Last Picture Show* but it is dealt with honestly and, as the saying goes, in the best possible taste. Still, Cybill Shepherd's poolside striptease remains one of the enduring memories for many who have seen the film.

The atmosphere of the movie was greatly enhanced by a background of songs by Hank Williams and a few other country singers from that era. The stark black and white photography helped to emphasize that the setting was a town that had seen much better days.

I don't know why but whenever I see *The Last Picture Show* I suddenly develop a craving for a Dr. Pepper.

Peter Bogdanovich, former film critic and film historian, is often accused of borrowing a bit too much from the work and techniques of other directors and this is, to some extent, valid. But at least he borrowed wisely, at least as far as *The Last Picture Show* was concerned.

In 1990, Bogdanovich directed and co-wrote – again with McMurtry – a sequel to *The Last Picture Show* called *Texasville* which featured about half a dozen stars from the original film playing the same roles some years later. Like too many sequels, this one was not a good idea and aroused little enthusiasm among audiences. It was also made in color so Bogdanovich was unable to even recapture the mood of the earlier picture. It was, however, typical of the uneven quality of Bogdanovich's career. He showed so much promise with *The Last Picture Show* but fulfilled only a small part of it.

===================================

YOUNG FRANKENSTEIN – 1974

In the 1970s, writer and director (and sometimes actor) Mel Brooks reintroduced a zaniness to the movies that had not been seen since the heyday of the Marx Brothers. It began in 1968 with *The Producers,* a film so off the wall and irreverent that few knew what to make of it and it played to mostly empty houses until Brooks' later successes revived interest in it. In 1974, Brooks produced two gems, both parodies of beloved film genres: the cowboy flick *Blazing Saddles* and the horror spoof *Young Frankenstein* which remains a true classic. Sadly, Brooks never hit those heights again as his output became increasingly uneven. Like too many film makers, his early works were his best.

Young Frankenstein was actually the brainchild of its star Gene Wilder who brought the idea to Brooks and then co-wrote the screenplay with him. In many ways, the movie is as much a Wilder creation as a Brooks one and, perhaps because of this, contains a more coherent plot than is found in many Brooks pictures. Wilder described the Brooks method of movie making: "We were not interested in polite titters, we want the audience rolling on the floor and falling about. Mel works on his feet – it's hit and miss, hit and miss, hit and miss. Then in the editing he will take out all the misses."

While *Young Frankenstein* sends up the classic horror movies of the Thirties, it does so with some degree of affection even going so far as to use the laboratory set from the 1931 version that starred Boris Karloff. Thus the film looked good even when trying to be ridiculous.

Wilder was fantastic in the title role as the grandson of the original Dr. Frankenstein who inherits his castle and his notebooks and eventually decides to create a creature of his own. His deadpan insistence on pronouncing the name of Frankenstein differently is a delight in the early scenes. But once he makes his fateful decision, Wilder goes completely into manic mode as only he could.

Peter Boyle made a memorable monster with a wider range of facial expressions than the monster usually had. Cloris Leachman was over the top as the grandfather's former mistress, Teri Garr was delightfully spacey as the buxom peasant girl who Wilder finds hard to resist, and Madeline Kahn was her usual outrageous self as Wilder's fiancée. Kahn was a regular in films by Brooks. She said: "Mel is sensual with me. He treats me like an uncle – a dirty uncle." There was even an unbilled cameo for Gene Hackman as a blind hermit. But Kenneth Mars, so good as the Nazi in *The Producers,* fails to make the same impact in *Young Frankenstein.*

The most inspired piece of casting was British comic Marty Feldman as Frankenstein's wild-eyed and hump-backed ("What hump?") hereditary assistant Igor. He brought a whole other dimension of craziness to the picture with both physical and verbal comedy, including ad-libs. Multiple re-takes were often required because of Feldman's antics and Wilder's habit of corpsing.

So far as Mel Brooks was concerned, there was never any question of making *Young Frankenstein* in black and white. After all, the classic horror movies it was spoofing were black and white pictures – color could not recapture the same aura. The studio took a lot of convincing, feeling that black and white was box office poison in 1974.

Young Frankenstein was a hit with audiences and helped Brooks and Wilder secure a long term contract with 20th Century Fox. Wilder, who had writing ambitions, began to work independently of Brooks and even tried his hand at directing several of his films. Brooks continued to make movies in his own inimitable style, some of which were also parodies of popular film genres. In 2007, following the success of his *The Producers* musical on Broadway, he turned *Young Frankenstein* into a reasonably successful musical.

Not everyone appreciated the sort of movies that Brooks and some of his imitators were making. Morose actor Jason Robards claimed to not find anything funny in *Young Frankenstein* and described it as high school humor. Veteran film maker Joseph L. Mankiewicz went even further, saying Hollywood was being killed by the twin evils of special effects and Mel Brooks. Luckily, these were minority opinions.

==================================

IN CONCLUSION

By the end of the 1960s, the production of black and white movies had virtually ceased. The theory was that people would be reluctant to leave their color televisions to pay to see a black and white film. In the 1970s, everything on television was in color, including commercials, so why not movies? It would be a brave or very persuasive director who would be able to make a movie in black and white after that.

There had been a few attempts to mix color with black and white. Lindsay Anderson's anarchic and somewhat surreal *If...* in 1968 featured black and white sequences in a color film for no apparent reason. A couple of black and white films, *The Picture of Dorian Gray* in 1945 and *The Solid Gold Cadillac* in 1956, both featured final shots in full color. The gimmick was not popular. Audiences felt that if one scene could be in color, why not the whole movie.

From time to time there were a few notable black and white pictures. *The Elephant Man* in 1980 used black and white to good effect as did Tim Burton with his marvelous *Ed Wood* in 1994. Steven Spielberg insisted on making *Schindler's List* a black and white film in 1993 although he cheated a little bit.

Black and white movies are a lost art form but thankfully interest in them is constantly being revived by people who love good movies. Many have been remastered to their former glory for DVD and occasional theater showings. If this book has inspired anyone to seek out some of these wonderful films, then I have done my job.

==

ABOUT THE AUTHOR

David Kaye was born in Baltimore in 1948. He first started to write short stories in elementary school and soon progressed to writing the scripts for his high school's annual spring musicals. Having been bitten by the theater bug, he went on to work at several regional repertory theaters as an assistant stage manager, a sometime actor and the author of workshop productions. Later on, he wrote film and music reviews for *The Chesapeake Weekly Review.* Since moving to the UK in 1984, he has written plays for BBC Radio, revue skits and occasional magazine articles. Some of his poems were translated for publications in a Russian poetry magazine. He has recently returned to writing with renewed inspiration, producing some novellas, books of personal recollections, and several books about movies. He now lives near London with his English wife Diane and their eccentric cat Willow.

===

Going to the Movies in Baltimore 1950s-1970s

An Affectionate Memoir

DAVID KAYE

Forgotten Films Of The Fifties

Looking Back At Overlooked Movies

DAVID KAYE

=================================

Quirky Movies Of The Sixties

A Wallow In Film Nostalgia

DAVID KAYE

=====================================

Memorable Movies of the Seventies

Films from a Weird and Wonderful Decade

DAVID KAYE

Printed in Great Britain
by Amazon